CHRISTIAN ADVICE

FROM
HIS
WIFE

WIFE
TESTED

HUSBAND
APPROVED

TO
HER
HUSBAND

By Tiffany Kameni

CHRISTIAN ADVICE ___FROM HIS WIFE TO HER HUSBAND__

TIFFANY KAMENI

ANOINTED FIRE CHRISTIAN PUBLISHING

PRAYER & DEDICATION

First and foremost, I must acknowledge you, FATHER GOD. You have been my reference, my focus, and my Teacher. You have taken me on this life's journey, and you have never left me behind. There were times when I went away from you to follow my own selfish desires. Despite my rebellion, you have always given me grace, and received me back into your open arms. You have washed me new again, and purged me of all of the sinful ways and sinful thinking that rebellion had placed on and in me. JEHOVAH, you are my everything. No man, place, thing, or situation can replace you. FATHER, I love and adore you because of who you are. Thank you for the lessons you have given me through this life's journey of mine. I commit to glorifying your Name in all that I do. You are worthy of all the praise, and I worship and adore you.

FATHER, I ask that you let the content of this book minister to the men (and women) of GOD who are married or plan to be married. FATHER, I ask that you open the understanding of everyone that reads this book. FATHER, glorify thy Name throughout this book, and in every word in this book. Thank you for revelation, and thank you for the information you have given me to write this book. I commit to continuing to spread the gospel in everything that I do. I love you and I bless your holy Name.
In CHRIST JESUS Name I pray...
Amen.

Your daughter,
Tiffany Kameni

TESTIMONIALS

Over the years, I have come across many books that are geared towards teaching women how to be better wives, but not very many books that instruct men on how to be better husbands. This book was like a breath of fresh air to my soul. All I could do was say "Amen" out loud through every chapter. As a married woman, some of the thoughts, feelings, and emotions I've had are perfectly described throughout the text. I wish I could place this book in the hands of every married man or soon to be married man I know. This book is scriptural yet the concepts are so easy to grasp. Even a new believing husband can take these principles and apply them to his marriage. I pray that every Christian man who can't seem to understand his wife would pick up a copy of this book. Their marriage will be sure to blossom quickly into the beautiful union it was intended to be.

-JASMINE BLAIR-

I must say Mrs. Kameni, if I had a thousand tongues, I couldn't tell you enough how much I've enjoyed this book. I absolutely love it. It has truly ministered to me. I can't tell you how much it's opened my eyes to so many needs and thoughts and emotions that my wife may have. I will also say that this is honestly the very first book, besides school books or my Bibles, that I've ever used a highlighter in. I'm so blessed that GOD created an intersection for our paths. God bless you and your ministry woman of GOD. And everything that you lay hands to in the future. It's my prayer that this work lands in every home, hut, igloo and apartment on the earth. Be blessed. You have truly blessed me.

-PAUL MILLER-

Hi Tiffany. I so enjoyed the book! It was revelatory and insightful; I didn't want to stop reading it, but most importantly to me as a wife, I would like see this book be a teaching tool for couples before they marry. Even the more, a beautiful wedding gift: his and hers! GREAT JOB!!

-D'ANDRA KING-RIVERS-

Tiffany,
First things first, I am so Godly proud of the way that you allow God to speak through you. This book was worth my time reading! As you know, I am also married to an African man (such a blessing). At times, while reading, I would say, "Honey, listen to this." He would listen, and his response would be "I just prayed about this or that to the Lord." Next his response was, "I don't know who wrote that book, but they are going to bless many marriages." I must say that I am absolutely grateful that you allowed me to review your book. Thank you again for all that you do in the Kingdom of God!

-PASTOR KHADIJAH RUCKER-DADDAH-

In marriage, there is much for each party to know. Sadly, we spend more time focused on the flaws and the past of our mates rather than the "HOW TO FIX" the present and future section of life. In this book, Tiffany has heard from God and relayed to the reader the "HOW TO" instructions to a Godly relationship with your spouse. Had this been written by a secular author, it may have been titled "Marriage for Dummies." The application through revelation for me has been life changing; simple, but life changing. This book is a MUST-HAVE for every man who sits and wonders why he is not progressing in the things of God. If you are married, check your marriage. If you are are thinking about marriage, THINK AFTER YOU HAVE READ THIS BOOK! This book may be the best little book a man or woman will ever pick up if they truly desire to have the marriage the way God designed it ....
GUESS NO MORE; READ THIS BOOK.

-DR. PRESTON DAVIS SR.
SENIOR PASTOR OF ST. MARY UNITED
F.W.B.C.
MCCOMB, MS-

I just got done reading the book! I tell you it was sooooo good that I woke up at 3:48 a.m. Friday morning and read a couple of pages! This book is A MUST-HAVE FOR ALL COUPLES!!! Those that are in the dating stages, newlyweds, as well as the seasoned married folk! If they read the content of this book, take it and apply it to their marriage; I'M CERTAIN IT WILL KEEP A LOT OF CHRISTIANS OUT OF DIVORCE COURT AND BRING

RESTORATION BACK TO THE LIFELESS
MARRIAGE! I am a Christian wife of 21 years this
November 2013... I met my husband at the age of 17
and married him at 21. We are both 42 now, and I
seriously wish this book was around then. I'm sure it
would've saved us both a lot of heartache & pain!
-NIECY COLLINS-

I read the book and totally enjoyed it. It opened my
eyes to certain things my better half was going
through. I felt that this came along at the right time
in our relationship and I will be doing my best to
apply the lessons in the book to better my
relationship with her.
-CHRISTOPHER LOTT-

I'm a currently a single and this book has blessed me
so much! It gave me insight into what to be as a wife
as well as what to expect from my husband. This
book gives straight-forward, insightful wisdom on
how to effectively know what God requires in a
marriage and how to please one another. Whether
you are married or single, this book is for you!

-DAVINIA GORDON-

Intro

First, let me state this. This book is NOT a man bashing book. This book is an educational read designed to build up marriages so that the lack of knowledge can stop tearing them down.

In this book, I'm your sister who helps you to understand what you may not understand. My goal is to be that voice that says what is right and what is wrong, without having to be affiliated with neither you nor your wife. This means that I'm neutral.

This book is simply an educational read put together to help the men of GOD in their marriages.

As a wife and a mentor, I have spoken with many wives about the issues in their marriage over the course of my life and ministry. What I have found is that many of the issues that plague one woman's marriage are the same issues that plague just about every woman's marriage.

In this book, I will teach you more about your wife and her design. Some of the issues that arise in marriage come in because of lack of knowledge. And this lack of knowledge doesn't just come from the husband, but many women enter marriage with no knowledge of how to be a wife and an unwillingness to learn.

What we learn is that every creature has a behavior that is characteristic of that creature. Men have certain behaviors, and women have certain behaviors. Then, add individuality on top of that, and you have a whole new breed of creature. Therefore, every woman, while similar, is not the same. But, when you don't know the characteristic of the creature, you can't properly care for it. You can't feed a cat dog food, and you can't place your dog in an aquarium because it's not a fish. All the same, a woman of GOD has a design that has to be fueled before she can properly operate as a wife.

Knowledge is power, and in this book, you will get past the long talks and get straight to the knowledge that you need to keep peace in your marriage, keep strife away from your marriage, and keep the fire burning in your marriage.

This is about being a wife...from a wife's point of view.

Table of Contents

-Chapter 1-

The Difference Between a Woman and a Wife

One of the biggest misconceptions around is that every decent woman is fit to be a wife, and this is simply not true. This is because we define words differently than GOD defines them. As human beings, we are often willing to settle for anything we consider "good enough" or "decent." We often do this when we are anxious or when we are trying to fill a void in our lives. This means that the very foundation of our desires is ungodly, since we are commanded not to be anxious for anything.

With that being said, you must know that there is a difference between a woman and a wife before you even start your search. If you don't learn the difference before you get married, the lesson will come to you while you are married. No man wants to live in a home where he can't find peace, and no woman wants to be married to a man who doesn't know how to usher peace in.

Just what is the difference between a woman and a

wife? Proverbs 18:22 reads, *"Whoso findeth a wife findeth a good thing, and obtaineth favour of the LORD."* If you will notice, the scripture did not read "Whoso findeth a woman." It read, "Whoso findeth a wife." Why is this distinction important? Of course, we already know that a wife is a woman, but what makes her different? A woman is born, but a wife is born again. In the same, when a woman is born again, she is no longer a mere woman, but she is a new creature in CHRIST. Once she has been cleaned up and her mind has been renewed, she is then hidden in the LORD. She is like a treasure, and many men will attempt to court her, but she is only the helpmate of one man. As long as she stays in obedience, she is hidden, and she awaits your arrival. It takes you, as the man, to go through the very same process of being saved, delivered, restored, and renewed before GOD will give you the directions to find her. In the meantime, you will run across several women, many of them even being women of GOD, but they are not anointed to be your helpmate. You will even come across wives in waiting who are anointed and appointed to be the helpmate of another man, but obedience will keep you from them. The misconception with many people in church is that anyone who is saved has the potential to be their spouses.

When I was a mere woman, I was a man's worst nightmare because I had a big mouth with no wisdom. I had a desire to be a wife, but no understanding of how to be a wife. I had a list of rules that life had taught me, but no knowledge of what GOD said. I believed in my heart that I would make a great wife, but the truth was that any man who dared to marry me wouldn't have found a wife because I wasn't hidden. They would have found a woman, and when you marry a woman, she doesn't become a wife; she becomes a married woman.

How do you know when a woman of GOD is your wife? The answer is simple. When GOD tells you. There will be many women who come your way, and to your "right now" way of thinking, they would make great wives. But, you have to understand if GOD hasn't revealed the location of your wife to you, you are still being cleaned up, or your wife is being prepared for her new role. This means that who and what are you today isn't necessarily who and what you'll be tomorrow. Your wife has to be able to merge through the dimensions of time with you, embracing who you are everyday. But, if you marry the wrong woman, she will always want the man whom you were yesterday, and she'll complain about who you are becoming. This is because she wasn't designed for you. She was designed to accompany another man as his wife, but you married her, and she didn't have the right tools to be your wife.

Listen for GOD, and don't allow yourself to be pulled out of HIS will by anxiety or your flesh's lustful demands. If you want to find a wife, you have to search the heart of GOD. Please understand that everything has a season, and every season has a reason. An apple tree doesn't grow up in one day; an apple tree can take anywhere from 3-15 years to mature. Even then, if you pick the apples while they are still green, they will be bitter. The same goes for a wife. If you pick her while she's out of season, she will be bitter.

A wife has to blossom and first be called a wife before you can obtain favor for finding her. If you find a woman, don't expect the favor of GOD to rest upon your marriage, and definitely don't expect her to be a good thing. She can only be what she is at that very moment. In addition, you may come across the woman who is anointed to be your wife, but if you pick her before her season is upon her, you will have to endure some pretty hard times as she goes through the process of preparation. One of my most quoted stories is my testimony of when I owned two Siberian Huskies. My male dog was two years old, and my female was a new addition to my home. She had begun to go into heat, and I wanted to breed her, so I researched information about breeding. I found a breeder who warned me not to breed her while she was six months old. She told me that breeding her at that age would not only stunt her growth, but her puppies could possibly die in her womb or be deformed. I thought that when a dog went into heat, they could be bred because they were considered adults, and I was right. They CAN be bred during their first heat, but they SHOULDN'T be bred.

If you end up taking a woman before she matures into a wife, you can stunt her growth as well because you will remove her from the transition of becoming a wife and bring her into a role of actually being married. Then, you will automatically expect her to assume the role of being a wife, and she wasn't yet called to be a wife because she was out of season. Therefore, she won't be able to successfully fill her role as the helpmate whom you need, but she will be able to perform some wifely duties, and this just isn't enough.

If you aren't married yet, ask the LORD to make you a husband. Just like a woman has to be anointed in the proper season as a wife, a man has to be anointed in the proper season as a husband. It is then and only then that his feet will touch the path to locate his wife. Until then, he'll run into many women who'd like a shot at being his married woman. Divorce court is full of married men and married women who don't want to be married anymore because they could not handle the role of a husband or a wife. They ran into the GOD-ordained covenant of marriage and got ran back out of it by their own flesh. Ask GOD to prepare you for your new role and to prepare your wife for her new role.

If you are married, ask the LORD to change you from being a married man to being a husband, and to change your woman from being a married woman to being a wife. Even if you picked her while in your disobedience, GOD can still recreate a new heart in her and assign her the role of accompanying you as a helpmate. If you picked the wrong one, or if you picked the right one in the wrong season, you will still have to endure her flesh as she is changed. In the same, she will still have to endure your flesh as you are changed. If the both of you can understand just where you are, you can come together and figure out how to make the transition a lot easier.

-Chapter 2-

Esther or Vashti

If you know the story of Esther, you would know
that King Xerxes was first married to Queen Vashti.
They threw a banquet, and King Xerxes got drunk
and sent for Vashti to come forward and show
herself. Queen Vashti was beautiful and her
husband was proud to show her off, but the queen
refused to come to him. Of course, just like any
red-blooded man, the king was humiliated. The
worst thing that a wife can do to her husband is to
get puffed up around his friends and colleagues.
Anyhow, he sought counsel about the matter, and
the princes advised him that he needed to forbid
Vashti from ever coming in his presence again, and
he was to marry a woman more suited to be a
queen. Queen Vashti was given a position lower
than a concubine, but she wasn't put out of the
castle. As her husband, King Xerxes followed the
law of not putting her away (divorce), but he simply
forbade her from having the highest role allotted to
a king's wife, and that is to be queen.

As with tradition, they sent out a royal decree

throughout the kingdom that every man is to be ruler of his household. (Of course, this was the King's attempt to, as we say, "save face.") A search was then made for a woman more suited for a king. Many women were brought to the castle, and according to the scriptures, they were all beautiful virgins. Each woman had to go through more than a year of preparation before she was allowed to come into the King's chamber. *"Before a young woman's turn came to go in to King Xerxes, she had to complete twelve months of beauty treatments prescribed for the women, six months with oil of myrrh and six with perfumes and cosmetics. And this is how she would go to the king: Anything she wanted was given her to take with her from the harem to the king's palace. In the evening she would go there and in the morning return to another part of the harem to the care of Shaashgaz, the king's eunuch who was in charge of the concubines. She would not return to the king unless he was pleased with her and summoned her by name"* (Esther 2:12).

Each woman, after sleeping with the king, was sent away to the concubine's chambers. This is because after sex, a woman was not (and still really isn't) considered a single woman. She was considered a married woman because ritual doesn't unite two people as one; sex does. Therefore, any woman whom the king slept with became his concubine, but the concubine wasn't good enough to be a wife. Her role was to please the king's flesh, but the wife's role was to be a helpmate. A helpmate to a king would undoubtedly have to be a queen, and not just any woman is equipped to handle such a role. Queen Vashti definitely wasn't equipped for the role.

When Esther's turn came to go into the king, she took only what Hegai (the king's eunuch) suggested that she take. The question that most ask is, "Did King Xerxes have sex with Esther before calling her queen?" Traditionally, the king would first hold a feast to announce his decision, and then the consummation would be done whenever the king pleased. Nevertheless, the Bible makes it clear that Esther was still a virgin when King Xerxes crowned her as queen. As a matter of fact, the Bible never even made mention of King Xerxes ever "knowing" Queen Esther, or better yet, having sex with her. It tells us that he made her queen; that's it. In those days, it wasn't abnormal for a man to betroth a woman to himself and to never sleep with her. For example, when King David got old, the Bible tells us that he couldn't keep warm. A search was made to find a virgin to keep him warm, and they brought him back Abishag a Shunammite. According to the scriptures (1 Kings), David didn't sleep with her. Again, there is no proof that King Xerxes had intercourse with Esther, nor is there any mention of any children being born to the couple, but that is irrelevant. Esther 2:17-20 reads: *"Now the king was attracted to Esther more than to any of the other women, and she won his favor and approval more than any of the other virgins. So he set a royal crown on her head and made her queen instead of Vashti. And the king gave a great banquet, Esther's banquet, for all his nobles and* *officials. He proclaimed a holiday throughout the provinces and distributed gifts with royal liberality. <u>When the virgins were assembled a second time</u>, Mordecai was sitting at the king's gate. But Esther had kept secret her family background and nationality just as Mordecai had told her to do, for she continued to follow Mordecai's instructions as she had done when he was bringing her up." (NIV)*

Where is your queen? Is she still hidden in the LORD or have you married her already? Unlike the days of old, it is not right for you to send your wife away and take a new one. Having been married twice, one time as a woman, and now as a wife; I have found that some men will still send you away for a period of time when things aren't at their best. Of course, your husband won't send you away from the house, but many men will distance themselves from you emotionally when you (the wife) are being overly emotional, and this is pure torture to a woman.

What if you married a Vashti? Could you just send her away from you and find yourself an Esther? Could you just punish her by withdrawing yourself emotionally from her, and leaving her to run herself crazy until she decided to finally submit to your demands? If you have married a Vashti, it could mean that you are like King Xerxes. King Xerxes was a pagan, but Esther was a woman of GOD. Her purpose with King Xerxes was only to save the Jews. She was anointed for that time to arise and become the king's queen. Therefore, being a Xerxes isn't something to brag about. Remember, he sent for Vashti when he was intoxicated just to show off her beauty. Even though she was wrong for not coming forward, she was a woman responding to a man. That's how women deal with men; they often go down to their level to relate to them. The only reason that this story made its way into the Bible was to tell the story of how the Jews were saved by the hand of GOD through a faithful woman of GOD.

To deal with a Vashti, you must first become a David. When a man rises up in his place as a man of GOD, his wife has to come up to where he is to relate to him. You have to govern your home the way that GOD told you to and not be moved to act like a mere man. In your obedience, GOD will deal with the woman whom you have married; and if she refuses to submit to HIM through you, HE will decide the just punishment for her. You should never take it upon yourself to try to punish your wife by removing yourself emotionally from her. Even though this punishment is harsh to most women, it won't work out in your favor because you are dealing with a woman as a man. As such, you will have to be demoted back to being a flesh-driven man in order to deal with her. You have to deal with a woman as a husband, and if she's not fit to be a wife, she will decide whether or not she wants to submit to the change required to be your wife. If she decides that she enjoys being a woman, take the lesson from it, and let GOD lead you in your dealings with her.

If you find that you are a man attracted to Vashti spirits, this is a clear indication that your heart is perverted. Perverted does not necessarily mean to be sexually twisted; perverted means that you are working opposite of how GOD designed you to work. Rather than trying to feed this mindset, you need to submit your heart to CHRIST so that it can be renewed by the changing of your mind. Men who find themselves attracted to rebellious women are themselves rebellious. It doesn't matter if they are in church or not in church; their heart is not turned to GOD. Their mouths may be speaking all things GOD, but their actions will reflect what their heart truly believes.

CHAPTER 3

The Inner Workings of a Wife

Women are builders by nature. GOD created us to be this way. Women are creatures of spontaneity. One day, we can be sweeping the living room, and the next day we can decide that we want new flooring for the living room. We are not created to stay comfortable in a certain setting for too long. Instead, we often get bored with our surroundings and want to change things up a bit. Men, on the other hand, are creatures of habit who get comfortable with things just as they are. Men like to leave things as they are and are often angered by a woman's desire to change things around. My husband is a great example. He uses our living room ottoman as his personal desk, and he often has all kinds of paperwork scattered on the ottoman. This bothers me, of course, because I am a creature of organization. I like things to be in order at all times. I would leave his papers sitting there for a week or more, never bothering them because I know that he may still be working on them. But, after a week of seeing him not touch the papers; I usually organize them and put them away and this drives him to the brink of insanity. He often tells me to leave things as they are, but at the same time, I know that if I did, our house would be a huge mess. Therefore, I try to negotiate with him, and he has gotten better with putting things away.

Women are creative in whatever they are anointed to do. When a woman has discovered her gifts and is operating in them, you will find that she's a cheerful woman. Why is this? Because she is functioning the way that she was designed to function. But when a woman has not discovered her gifts, she can be needy, demanding, and aggressive. This is because she is designed to move, but she's being still. If the Earth stopped moving today, all life in it would perish. The circulating of the Earth sets a lot of things in motion, from the greatest of things to the smallest. Everything in the Earth is tied to the Earth's movement.

As a woman, we are like little earths, and everything in us is tied to our movements. When we are busy doing what we were created to do, we give life to everything we apply our hearts and hands to. When we are not busy doing what we were created to, we take life away from anything we apply our hearts and hands to. That's why a woman who is not in purpose can be spiritually draining to have. Can you imagine pulling up to your own home and not wanting to get out of the car because of a contentious woman? Every day that you come home, she is complaining about something or someone. That's what happens when a woman's build has been altered by soul ties, unforgiveness, or a lack of purpose.

Women are creatures of vision. We spend a lot of time in our imaginations, planning out our futures. In the same, we often spend time seeing things that we don't want to see in our imaginations. As a result, we will proactively try to prevent those things from happening. For example, let's say that your brother was coming into town, and he was going to be staying at your house for a week. Your brother is a playboy and does not respect women. Your wife begins to seem a little less happy since she heard the news, and she becomes more and more withdrawn. Finally, she lets it out. She's not happy about him coming to visit, but she doesn't offer up a solution. She's hoping that you will take the lead and not allow your brother to stay in your home. Now, you may be saying that a wife that makes such a request or even thinks that way is not a good wife, but quite the contrary. Bad association ruins useful habits. Your wife is your helpmate, and one of her roles is to be a visionary in your marriage. Men often walk one foot in front of the other, never taking consideration for the steps ahead. But women tend to think ahead and prepare accordingly. This is what makes a husband and a wife a great team when they are in CHRIST. A wife will guard her marriage like a lioness guards her cubs. When she senses danger ahead, she will react accordingly. Even in the lion kingdom, the male lions rarely fight off other male lions trying to take their territories. The females often gang up and attack these intrusive males because they know that the male will not only kill the leader of the pack, but he will also kill all of the young so that he can mate with the females.

Women can come off as insensitive when the husband is still young in experience, but as he wisens up, he will almost always agree with his wife. That's because he will discover over time that his wife's intentions were not bad. When a man is young, he will often think that his wife's intentions are selfish and rooted in insecurity, but this isn't always the case. A woman is designed to protect her young, and when the king isn't protecting the castle, the queen will step up to the plate until he's back on board. My marriage makes a great example. In the beginning, my husband didn't completely trust my intentions, and I saw that. I saw intruders trying to place a breech in our marriage, and I responded aggressively. Now, my husband didn't see them as intruders because they were related to him, but I saw their true colors. I wasn't blinded by familiarity; I was looking at the fruit. In addition, my husband wanted to befriend everyone whom he came in contact with, and I was against this. He's from Cameroon, so he didn't understand that a bad person could smile at you and hold a conversation with you. He thought that anyone that was nice to him was a decent person. I'm American, on the other hand. I know the people here. I know that there are some good people, and there are many bad ones. I've experienced people helping me out with one hand, all the while stabbing me in the back with their other hand. Therefore, I was completely against his openness. At first, he challenged me often, and we argued to the point where we were considering a divorce. He didn't like how closed-minded I was towards new relationships and family, and I didn't like how open-hearted he was towards people and family.

One day, I went to get my hair braided by a Nigerian girl. I'd found her on Craigslist, and I traveled down to Tampa to her house to get my hair done. Anyhow, the transition was finalizing. I was now a wife, but my old way of thinking was fighting for its life. The girl and I began talking, and I discovered that she was a Christian woman. I was happy about this, and we began to talk about our roles as wives. She was married to an American man, and I was married to an African man. I started telling her about my husband's insistent desire to fit in with others, and his family ties. I was tired of fighting with him about the matter, and I didn't understand why he couldn't see what I was seeing. The girl spoke something to me that I knew had come from Heaven's throne. She told me that I needed to let him see for himself. It was not my place to hold him up or be his crutch. I'd made bad choices before, and through the consequences that followed, I learned my lessons. He needed the same opportunity to learn and grow. You see; he'd spent his years in college while I spent my years in the real world. I took her advice, and I stopped challenging him. It was out of order and against my design to challenge my husband. I even found that a lot of my frustration didn't come from what he was doing; it came from me going against my design trying to stop him from falling in the trap that I saw ahead. When I stepped back and let GOD be GOD, it didn't take him long to learn. He got burned a couple of times by friends and family, and he learned the lesson for himself. I didn't rub his nose in it; I just let him tell me about the lesson, and I sat there as a student willing to learn even more from his mistakes.

I was going against my design to challenge him, and this was frustrating me. It was and is not my place to challenge my husband; I had to learn that. If your wife is challenging you often, it's not always because she wants your position. There are many factors that cause a woman to not trust her husband's leadership, and they include:

- Unbroken soul ties. (On her part or yours.)
- Unforgiveness.
- Lack of trust due to something the husband has done.
- Lack of trust due to something the husband is doing. <Current.>
- Lack of trust due to something the wife has done.
- Lack of trust due to something the wife is doing. <Current.>
- Poor leadership. <It's the truth uncut.>
- Rebellion. <Of course, rebellion is witchcraft.>
- Lack of knowledge.

Whatever the issue, you have to get to the root of it, and pull up the root.

Never try to "fix" a woman. Women were created in such a way that we cannot even understand one another wholly. We can relate to one another, for the most part; but we don't understand other women entirely. That's why many women don't like to have female friends. It's hard enough for us to deal with our own issues, but to add another emotional creature's issues on the pile can be too much for many women.

Let's say that your wife is a little too strong for you. You want your wife to be a little quieter and less aggressive. Nevertheless, the wife you have is not even considering this role that you are trying to fit her for, and this has caused many arguments between the two of you. Take this into consideration:

GOD may have designed her to be a strong woman, and this is all that she can be. Now, when her heart isn't right before HIM, she may channel her aggression in the wrong way towards the wrong people. Of course, this would be a major issue because no one wants to be on the other end of an aggressive and ungodly woman. But trying to rewire her mind won't solve the issue. Instead, that would only make things worse because she can only function in the way that she was designed to function in. If she goes outside of her design, she won't have peace, and she won't be able to protect her young because she won't be able to identify with herself. That's a surefire way to send a woman to the crazy house. Your goal should be to understand her design and to pray for her deliverance if her heart isn't right. At the same time, you have to be the king of your castle and manage your home, no matter how aggressive she is. This is how you drive demons out of your home and away from your family. You stand in the gap as an intercessor, and you authoritatively run your home no matter what. *"But I would have you know, that the head of every man is Christ; and the head of the woman is the man; and the head of Christ is God"* (1 Corinthians 11:3).

You should NEVER grow weary trying to restore order in your home. If your wife is battling with a Jezebel spirit, you've got one fight on your hands, but obedience to CHRIST will cause you to win that fight if you faint not. (Pray about it and research the Jezebel spirit). Just don't get distracted by what you see and challenge her flesh; stay focused on the spiritual aspect of it, and fight for your wife. You're not the only one under attack in this situation, but she is also under attack, along with your children. Jezebels hate order. How do you fight off a Jezebel? *"Submit yourselves therefore to God. Resist the devil, and he will flee from you"* (James 4:7).

Again, never try to rewire your wife's thinking because you just may be messing with how she is set up. She may have been designed to be the wife of another man, but you took her for a wife instead. If she was designed for someone else, she has the tools to aid that man in his journey. It is only normal that the two of you aren't merging well. In this case, you would have to repent and ask GOD to reassign her to you, since you've already married her. You cannot and should not attempt to change her. This is an error that always brings about negative results. Your goal is to obey GOD and continue on doing what HE has called you to do. Think about it; would you plant a seed today, yell it at tomorrow, and expect it to be a tree next week? No. You can only plant the seed and cultivate that seed often. You would have to water that seed and let the seasons play out. You don't possess the power to make that seed sprout into a tree. Neither do you possess the power to change your wife. "*So then neither is he that planteth any thing, neither he that watereth; but God that giveth the increase*" *(1 Corinthians 3:7)*. Appreciate your wife's design and let GOD be GOD. There is a process that you both must endure anytime elevation is on the horizon. This process includes a dying to self and the acquiring of the wisdom, knowledge, and understanding that you will need to possess in your new and elevated roles. Instead of becoming angry with one another when elevation rounds the corner, try embracing one another so that elevation won't be turned away by your separation.

If you find that your wife isn't happy, there may be a chance that she is simply not operating in her purpose. A car that doesn't move begins to rust; bread that isn't eaten begins to spoil; a river that isn't running begins to stagnate. She needs to move, and she needs to move in her purpose. Study your wife and you will see the evidence of who she is, if you don't already know. Provide her with the tools and support that she needs to go forward in her purpose, and you will see her blossom.

-CHAPTER 4-

<u>The Temperament of a Wife</u>

The temperament of a wife is directly linked to the design of the human part of her, but it also bears witness to who she really is. She may be quiet and passive; then again, she may be quiet but aggressive. Her temperament is linked to: her family, her current environment, the environment she's grown up in, her purpose in life, and her perception on life.

Family: We all know about generational curses. Whatever our parents battled with is oftentimes passed down to their children for generations to come. Sometimes, you may not even know your family's history and still fall into the very same mindsets that enslaved them. The familiar part of us is animalistic in nature. Just like animals, we develop structures, cultures, and beliefs that are not to be challenged. That's why when you witness a child who does not fit the mold of his or her family, they are often mistreated, talked about, and eventually cast out.

Your wife undoubtedly picked up a way of thinking

from her family, just like you picked up a way of thinking from yours. But, we have to submit our hearts to GOD so that these demonic and generational mindsets will flee from us. Even after we've been saved, delivered, and sanctified; you will still sometimes witness the residue of old thinking patterns.

Current Environment: As creatures, we have to adapt to our environments to survive. You will notice that your wife is happier and more energetic in certain environments, whereas she seems unhappy and drained in other environments. It's not always that she is trying to be difficult when you go into certain places; sometimes, she is just sensitive to what is in that environment. Let's say that every time you take your wife over to your Mother's house, she stops talking and doesn't act her normal self. This bothers you, of course, because you want her to get along well with your Mother. Instead of challenging your wife, you should ask her what it is that makes her behave this way. If she says that she is unsure, pray about it. She may be sensing that she isn't truly welcome there, but because it's your Mother in question, you won't test the environment or pay attention to the signs. Additionally, if you have moved to a new home and your wife seems unhappy there, try blessing the house. Remember this: Men are projectors, and women are receptors. A man will often set the stage for the atmosphere when he enters a place, but a woman will often sense what is in the atmosphere when she enters a place. Trust the GOD in her. Always communicate with her and ask her what she's feeling. If you notice that your wife's signals are picking up bad vibes, you need to stand in as the strongman and start binding up anything that is unlike GOD.

Past Environment: Our past environments play a major role in our current environments. Let's say that your wife was born and raised in a high-crime area. She learned how to survive in her neighborhood by paying attention to what was going on around her. Have you ever noticed that parents that have children in high-crime areas aren't afraid to send their children to the store? This is because the parents have adapted to the area and feel no sense of threat. They believe that the only people that are threatened in those areas are the criminals. Nevertheless, the parents will teach the children how to spot any signs of danger and to react accordingly. As we grow up, we don't lose this extra sense. Instead, we take it with us wherever we go.

Her Purpose In Life: Her purpose is directly linked to her design. She was designed for her purpose. That's why you will find that women have different temperaments that seem to go well with what they do for a living. For example, a woman who is an entrepreneur and is called to build won't be extremely passive. She can't be; otherwise, people would tear down whatever she attempts to build. She may be nice, and this may be mistaken as a passive personality, but when tried, you will find that she's anything but passive. It goes without saying, when a woman is in sin, you can still see her purpose on her. It's just perverted by her sin. *"For*

the gifts and calling of God are without
repentance" (Romans 11:29).

Her Perception On Life: A woman's perception on life is influenced by what she believes, and whatever is in her heart. For example, if she hasn't forgiven the people that have hurt her in her life, her perception will be shaped by her unforgiveness. If she has a rosy view of mankind, you will find that she's extremely loving, understanding, and non judgmental. Her perception can also be directly linked to you, the husband. If you were an awful man to her, she may begin to perceive men as awful creatures.

When a woman becomes a wife, her temperament begins to change. She has to assume her new role in life, and she will first have to adapt to that new role. That's why the first year of marriage is often the hardest on couples. Both parties are trying to merge their habits and beliefs, and this can be a trying experience. Her temperament is basically her substance (or what is in her) being made manifest outwardly.

One of the best things that you can do for your wife is to study her. Never try to change her to be the "type of woman" that you like because she's more than a woman; she's a wife. And she's not just a wife; she's an individual handmade by GOD and crafted to be who she is. I have witnessed so many men get married and try to change their wives into the characters they wish they'd married. Some men (and women alike) have an idea as to what they'd like in a spouse, but here's the thing: What you want isn't always what you need. You have no idea of what GOD has in store for you, and the wife whom HE has crafted for you is designed to go into your future with you and still function as you are shifted from one level to another. Those past women, on the other hand, were good for who you were back then. Just because a woman fit into your life like a puzzle piece some years ago doesn't mean she'd be a perfect fit for you today, or that she'd continue to be a perfect fit for you tomorrow. You should never focus on the right now man, but always focus on CHRIST and what HE has assigned you to do. Your assignment is your purpose, and any woman not assigned to be your wife cannot help you to complete your assignment because she doesn't have the tools or design to do so.

Even if you don't like your wife's temperament, learn to love her as she is and appreciate who she is. My husband and I often create small talk with elderly couples when we go out to eat. Jean always asks them the secret to their longevity in marriage, and the answer has ALWAYS been the same. Every man said that he learned to listen to his wife, and he learned to trust her. The temperament of these women has proven to be custom designed for her husband's destiny over the years. They were perfectly matched, even when they didn't know it! Just imagine had they gotten rid of these women some years ago and married another woman. They wouldn't have these testimonies; instead, they would probably have headstones somewhere with their names on it.

Again, appreciate your wife's design and appreciate the process of change that she will endure to aid you in your assignment.

-CHAPTER 5-

<u>Your Role Versus Her Role</u>

As the husband, GOD has already assigned you to a role, and HE has assigned your wife to a role in the union. Contention comes about when we try to reassign one another to roles that GOD did not assign us to, or when we try to take on roles that are not our own. Contention also arises when we don't respect the roles of one another.

One of the greatest misconceptions in marriage is that we are only here for our spouses, and that our purpose is wrapped up in our spouses. This is not true. Our duty is to fulfill the roles that GOD has assigned us to. In this, we will automatically respect and love our spouses as they should be respected and loved. When we make their roles all about us, we set ourselves up as idols, and any idol has to be destroyed. In addition, when we try to get our spouses to focus on serving our needs and brokenness, we are actually reassigning them with our directions. To follow our directions, they would have to disobey GOD'S directions.

As a husband, your role is to be a provider for and a protector of your family. GOD is the Great Architect, and HE has given you a blueprint of what HE wants you to build. Now, you won't see the whole picture at once, because GOD reveals more of the picture to you as you walk in fear and trembling of HIM. HE has assigned your wife to be your helpmate, but she isn't designed to help you in sin. She isn't designed to serve you; she is designed to serve the LORD by serving you. When you aren't in purpose, she isn't supposed to participate in your sin or your sinful thinking. Instead, she will challenge you. She will get out of order when you are not in order because her head is not properly being covered by you.

Now that you have the blueprint, you have to weather the storms and start building. Your wife's design is directly linked to that blueprint that the LORD has given you; therefore, your dreams will be her dreams. The two of you will passionately build what you were called to build if you're not battling against your purpose. Yet again, if she wasn't called to be your wife, and you married her anyway, she will have to be reassigned to you. Otherwise, she'll come to your structure with the wrong tools. This isn't to say that you should go out and marry the wrong woman, because this actually delays the building process. It doesn't take long for GOD to reassign her, but what takes a while is for her to walk in her new design when she's used to walking in her old design. It could take years or even decades for her to accept who she is and to stop trying to be who she was. When in change, women become emotional and sometimes insecure. This means that if you marry another man's wife, you will have to endure some situations that you weren't designed to endure; therefore, you will often have to ask the LORD to loan you HIS strength.

In marriage, we often try to reassign our spouses based on where we currently are. If we are undelivered from enslaved mindsets, we try to reassign our spouses to be wardens who let us out of our daily cages, or we will try to make our spouses cellmates that keep us company in our prisons. It is not easy to be married to a lost soul because lost people don't merge well with saved people. How can they? *"And the light shineth in darkness; and the darkness comprehended it not" (John 1:5).* A child of GOD cannot understand a child of the devil and vice versa, and it's a waste of time to try to understand one another in such a case. Instead, one of the two will have to convert to the place where the other resides. Prayerfully, the sinner is saved and submits his or her heart to GOD. But this doesn't happen frequently because it is easier to pull a man down than it is to lift him up. This means that it would be easier for a sinner to bring a saint down than it would be for a saint to lift up a sinner. Now, it's not impossible and the Bible tells us what to do when we are unequally yoked. The Saint can't leave the sinner, but the sinner can leave the Saint; therefore, if your spouse is not saved, you have to stick around and pray for them. Should they decide that they can't deal with you or your GOD anymore, you are commanded to let them walk. *"But to the rest speak I, not the Lord: If any brother hath a wife that believeth not, and she be pleased to dwell with him, let him not put her away. And the woman which hath an husband that believeth not, and if he be pleased to dwell with her, let her not leave him. For the unbelieving husband is sanctified by the wife, and the unbelieving wife is sanctified by the husband: else were your children unclean; but now are they holy. But if the unbelieving depart, let him depart. A brother or a sister is not under bondage in such cases: but God hath called us to peace. For what knowest thou, O wife, whether thou shalt save thy husband? Or how knowest thou, O man, whether thou shalt save thy wife?" (1 Corinthians 7:12-16)*

Your role is vital to the conception and birth of your purpose. Your wife's role is vital to the conception and birth of your purpose. Again, your purpose isn't to be her husband, and her purpose isn't to be your wife; but your purposes are from GOD. You are just accompanying one another in purpose. You are your wife's treasure, and she is your treasure. The more you do together for GOD, the better your marriage will be. A couple that is in purpose won't have much time to bicker. Now, a couple not in purpose will fight about anything underneath the sun because any time we are not operating in our designs, we are operating against them. Take a brush and brush your cat or dog's fur in the opposite direction of which it grows and watch their reaction. Your cat would probably scratch-slap you, and your dog would probably get up and get away from you. It's uncomfortable to them for their fur to be brushed against the direction in which it grows.

Think of your wife in the same manner. Anytime she is being groomed for purpose or in purpose, she will gladly submit to you. She will be at peace and she will have joy in her heart. But, when your wife is pushed against her purpose, she will respond negatively because she is not comfortable being pushed in the wrong direction. Who would be?

When you know your roles in CHRIST, and you operate in those roles, you will find peace, happiness and longevity. Instead of thinking how you can please your wife, try to find ways to please the LORD. In doing so, HE will command you to do certain things for your wife that HE knows that she wants and needs at any given time. Your role is to stay focused on pleasing the LORD, and everything will follow through.

-CHAPTER 6-

<u>She Wants to Wear the Pants</u>

This has got to be the number one complaint
amongst men. I have heard many men say that their
wives are trying to take their positions. In many
cases, it's true, and the wife has to humble herself or
be humbled by the hand of GOD. Then again, in
some cases, the problem isn't the woman wanting to
be the head of the house; the problem is the
husband's warped definition of what a man is and
what a man does. For example, as I mentioned
earlier, Jean is foreign. He is from a country called
Cameroon, and he had been in school practically his
whole life. We married right before he graduated
from college, so when we moved in together, there
was a lot that he didn't know. Me, on the other
hand, I'd been married before for seven years. I
knew the ins and outs of marriage, and I knew a lot
of what was expected of me. Anyhow, Jean didn't
like my independent streak when it came to doing
things around the house that he'd labeled "a man's
job." But, what was I to do? I would only get
hands-on with the things that he didn't know how to
do. For example, we'd purchased some new bar

stools one day, and the instructions were complicated. They were poorly written using terms that even I didn't understand, so I did what I knew how to do. I started putting the stools together based upon my knowledge. I'd worked at a local Wal-Mart for seven years when I was younger, and I had a little experience putting things together. Now, in my first marriage, I didn't show off those skills because I knew that he loved being the one who assembled furniture. So I acted naïve and let him have his moment. With Jean, however, I couldn't just sit back because he didn't have a clue as to how to put some things together. Therefore, we'd have to hire someone, and that wasn't happening on his pride's schedule.

Jean had attempted to put the bar stools together, but it wasn't working out. I knew that his English was limited and that the instructions were poor, so I got up and grabbed the second bar stool box. I opened it, and I began to put the stool together....successfully. He stopped working and started watching me. I could feel him getting upset, and I knew it was all rooted in his pride, but at the time, I felt that he'd just have to get over it. Well, it took him a few hours to get over it. I remember hearing his disappointed voice as I was working. "You want to be a man," he said with his strong accent. I laughed. Because I was learning how to be a wife, I began to challenge him with my pride. I was upset that he was upset. Was I wrong? Yes, in a way. I have since learned to let a man be what he defines as a man, and to let him make his mistakes so that he can learn. At that time, however, I just wanted my bar stools put together. Since then, he's learned a lot, and he now assembles everything by himself.

As you can see, in our case, Jean's pride got the best of him. His definition of what a man is and what a man does came roaring out when I tripped over his understanding. Therefore, saying that one's wife wants to be a man isn't always true. The question is: What do you define as the roles and responsibilities of a man, and what does she define as the roles and responsibilities of a man? Sometimes, you will find that your definitions are different; therefore, you will continue to clash until the both of you come to a mutual understanding and compromise.

Then again, there are the cases where some women actually do want to be the heads of their homes. Now, many of them won't verbalize this, but it shows in their actions. Of course, this is out of order, and it is rooted in witchcraft, for rebellion is witchcraft. In these cases, talking with your wife won't avail you much, because the root of the issue is much deeper than you can see. Many women who desire to take the lead in their marriages are fearful of something, so they try to take the wheel because they trust their own lead. Many times, this stems from them having some traumatic event in their lives. The worst part about trauma is that it always invites more trauma. People who were hurt and have not completely healed of the hurt they experienced continue to find themselves in situations where they are hurt again and again. One of the most common stories that I have heard women share is that of being molested as a child and then getting themselves into bad relationships where they were abused and abandoned. They'd find themselves in relationships behind relationships, and each time they were betrayed. Finally, they decided that enough was enough, and they took control of their lives. Then you came along and put a ring on their fingers. Therefore, in their marriages, they are determined to stay in control to ensure that they are not hurt again. These women need much more than what you can offer them. They need healing, and they need understanding.

Should you let your wife wear the pants until she gets the healing that she needs? No way! You shouldn't come against the wife, but come against that spirit that is fueling her up with lies. Come against fear. Have a heart-to-heart with her and get her to talk about the things that have happened to her, and whatever you do, don't make her feel judged. Women shut down when they feel judged because they fear that your views will change about them, and you'd walk away. I can tell you from experience that a woman who has been traumatized often has many things that she wants to tell you, but she has to feel comfortable sharing those things with you. If she feels insecure in her marriage, and she's not sure that it's going to last; she will clam up. If you present yourself as squeaky clean, she won't share those things with you because she doesn't want to come off as dirty.

Example: When I was young, I was molested a lot by different people; both men and women. When I became a young adult, my mind was perverted and my soul was abused. So, my view on men was perverted. I saw them as creatures that needed to be put on a leash and watched. I didn't trust men, but I did want the physical part of a man. I went from relationship to relationship, breaking up with every man who showed any characteristics of the men that had molested me. To me, I thought I was in control. I wasn't like my friends. I didn't cry about men because I didn't give my heart to them. Anyhow, the LORD had been dealing with my heart, and I finally began to surrender to HIM. But, I wasn't ready to be a wife just yet. Even though I'd given up clubbing, drinking, and doing every destructive thing to myself; my mind was still perverted. I was struggling to become the woman I knew I could be, and the LORD sent me to a wonderful church where HE began to feed me HIS WORD through my Pastor and Uncle. I could feel the changes being made in me as understanding came in, but I still wasn't ready yet. I was still nothing but a woman. Then I met a man, and because I was a baby Christian, I went back into fornication. The conviction was now present, however, so I couldn't remain in fornication. We talked about marriage, and finally, we decided to get married.

Before and after marriage, he grilled me again and again to reveal my sexual history to him, and I wasn't comfortable doing this. I was still ashamed of what I had been, and I only wanted to be seen for who I was. I finally started opening up one day just to quiet him, and once I mentioned man number five, I remember him saying, "No man wants to be with a woman who's been with more men than he has been with women." He'd told me about four people that he'd been with, and he claimed that was the whole list. So, naturally, I became ashamed and shut down, and I stayed quiet over the years.

Fast-forward to now. Of course, I got divorced, and I remarried. My husband now has never asked me about my past, but now I'm no longer ashamed about it, so I tell him how twisted I was. I tell him how bad the devil had my mind back then, and he witnesses me testifying to young women all the time. So, the shame is not there anymore, and it doesn't control me anymore. The past lost its power over me when I began to testify about it.

The message here is to be understanding, loving, and nurturing towards your wife. Let her know that no matter what she's done in her past, you will still love her, and you won't use it against her. If she's not comfortable sharing it with you today, that's okay. Be understanding and prepare yourself for the day that she will be willing to reveal it to you. Even better than that, tell her about your past and what you are ashamed of. When women see your scars, they are more likely to show you their own. Once she is free from the ghosts of her past, you will witness her becoming more submissive towards you. Because the very things that once controlled her have lost their power over her. And what's even greater is when she begins to share her testimony and help other women who were once like her.

With my husband, I feel that I don't have to be ashamed of who I was, but it did take me a while to start opening up to him. When he would embrace me and explain to me why I did the things I did, I felt that I could tell him anything, and this opened the door for me to share my story with the world.

Whatever is holding your wife hostage needs to be bound. Anytime the demons from our past are free to roam, they will bind us. Remember Matthew 18:18, *"Verily I say unto you, whatsoever you shall bind on earth shall be what has been bound in heaven: and whatsoever you shall loose on earth shall be what has been loosed in heaven."* Keep binding every demonic force that is attached to, attacking, or seducing your wife. I remember going through warfare training, and this man taught me something that I exercise to this very day. I told him how I was at a person's house binding up devils, and he said to me, "Okay, but where did you send them?" I replied that I'd cast them out of the house. He asked me again, "Okay, but where did you send them?" I didn't understand, but he followed through and said, "If I throw you out of a house; couldn't you get back in?" Finally, he told me, "Baby girl, you have to send them somewhere. Send them to the pit (or abyss) and bind them there 'til the day of Judgment." Since I learned this, I live in complete peace, because anytime I feel the enemy has sent one of his imps at me, I know what to do with them. In other words, I learned to battle against what I could not see.

Never give up your position as the head of the

house, because believe it or not, you aren't relinquishing that spot to your wife; if you submit to her, you are relinquishing your spot to devils. You're not fighting flesh and blood. Sure, you may see her standing there being combative, but the fight is a battle between righteousness and rebellion. GOD already established the order; therefore, we can't change it, even if we don't agree with it. The order is put in place to protect you and your family. *"But I would have you know, that the head of every man is Christ; and the head of the woman is the man; and the head of Christ is God" (1 Corinthians 7:3).* Look at the chart below to get a better understanding.

Correct Order
<ul><li>GOD</li><li>CHRIST</li><li>Man</li><li>Woman</li></ul>
With this order, you see that everyone is protected by GOD for HE is the Head.

Disorder
<ul><li>GOD</li><li>CHRIST</li></ul>   <ul><li>Woman</li><li>Man</li></ul> <ul><li>GOD</li><li>CHRIST</li></ul>

- Man

    - Woman

The woman is covered through the man, but if she isn't covered by her husband, she isn't covered by CHRIST, because CHRIST is the head of man. From the charts above, you can see that in both forms of disorder, the woman is left uncovered. When the husband, however, remained in line with the WORD, battling that rebellion in his wife, he remained covered, but she was uncovered as long as she was in rebellion. She chose to rebel, and this opened her up for the devils associated with rebellion. Now, in her husband's obedience, he will cause her to either get back under his covering, or she will flee from him to go and serve her rebellion full time. In this case, she is an unbeliever, and as such, he is required to let her leave. As long as the husband stays in line with CHRIST, his home will fall in order...with or without the wife.

Another form of disorder is listed below:

- GOD
- CHRIST
- Man and Woman

A lot of women want to have an equal place alongside their husbands, but this is out of order. She is your teammate, but your directions come from your head and you relay them to her. In addition, when she is obedient to GOD, HE will confirm directions to you through her.

Does this mean that you are to push your weight around? No. One thing about women is that when we know you are being led by GOD, it is easier for us to submit. But, if you start being led by your flesh or devils, most women won't follow you because they don't have to. How is that? CHRIST is the head of man. If CHRIST isn't your head, you are submitting to another authority. In such a case, the wife's job is now to remain obedient to GOD, and to win you with her chaste behavior. *(Read 1 Peter.)*

When your wife wants to wear the pants, take the time out to assess the situation. Don't just jump into the flesh and try to battle with her. Instead, ask yourself if it is your pride that makes you see it that way, and if so, how can you correct it. If it isn't your pride, but your wife is actually battling with you for your position, talk to your Head (CHRIST) and ask HIM what you are to do. Don't give her the role, no matter how angry she gets, because you are basically saying to the devils driving her that they are not allowed in your home.

CHAPTER 7

The Terrorist In Your Home

What is opposition? We know opposition to mean "to come against." The Free Dictionary defines opposition as, "The act of opposing or resisting." But just what are we going against? What are we opposing or resisting? Better yet, what is coming against us? What is opposing or resisting us?

Opposition is the opposing of one's position. It is to stand against the position of someone else. Opposition can be broken down into three words: Oppose, Opposite, and Position. So, anytime you witness opposition in your home, something or someone is opposing your position. But, just what is your position, and does it line up with the WORD of GOD.

We have two positions: One is the position that GOD has anointed us to fill, and two is our opinions or the positions that we want/ intend to fill. When our desires and plans do not match up with GOD'S plan for us, we are in the same opposing GOD. Anyone that opposes GOD will not have peace, because peace is a blessing from GOD. Peace is found when you go with GOD, but peace will never be found when you go against HIM. Therefore, when we feel an opposing coming from within, it is normally because we are not in position or we are opposing a new position that GOD is giving us.

Who is the terrorist in your home? The terrorist is the one who comes against the peace of that home. Quite understandably, the husband will say that his wife is the terrorist, and the wife will say that her husband is the terrorist. In both cases, however, the terrorist is usually both parties, because when we don't understand the position of our spouses, we oppose it.

Anytime we make a decision, we have taken a position for or against something. Let's say that your sixteen-year-old daughter wants to date, and you have settled in your position against her dating. You were once a young man, so you know what's in the head of a teenage boy. You also know that boys that age aren't looking for committed relationships, whereas young girls are. Your wife, on the other hand, wants to let her date because she can relate to how your daughter is feeling. She was once a young girl who had the same issue with her father, so her position is for your daughter dating. This means that the two of you are opposing one another's positions. How could you reconcile this? You reconcile this issue by agreeing with the WORD of GOD. Did GOD say that a man would leave his father and his mother and cleave to his girlfriend and the two shall be one flesh? No! Did

GOD say that men and women should test the waters before making a decision as to who they will marry? No! Therefore, the husband's position against the daughter dating is right because dating is not found in the WORD of GOD. In the same, the husband cannot be for his sixteen-year-old son dating as well. There is order in GOD'S Kingdom, and the two of you need to be for this order, not against it.

Then, there is the opposing of who GOD has called us to be. What if you married a woman who does not like your decision to pursue your dreams? She thinks it's stupid, and she verbally opposes you every time the conversation comes up. You're passionate about wanting to pursue these dreams; this is part of who you are, but she's gotten accustomed to who you were, and she doesn't welcome this sudden attempt at changing. This could mean one of the following:

1. You married the wrong woman and made her your wife. Again, a woman is designed to be with her husband, and if you weren't supposed to marry her, you took her illegally. Now, her design doesn't change just because you married her. You will have to repent and ask GOD to reassign her to you.

2. You married the right woman in the wrong season. What's harder than being married to the wrong spouse is being married to the right spouse in the wrong season. Sometimes, GOD will allow us to meet our spouses and our goal was just to get to know one another as friends. The season would come when the friendship blossomed into a marriage, but we are human. We want what we want when we want it; that is until we get what we get when we don't want it. A woman in the wrong season won't be much of a helpmate to you because she's still in transition. She won't understand your position because she wasn't called to understand it just yet. At any given rate, you have to repent and let the seasons play out.

3. You married the right wife in the right season, and she is just in rebellion or you are in rebellion. Satan doesn't stop working just because we married the right ones in the right seasons. As a matter of fact, it would give points to his team if he can destroy such a union and place doubt in the hearts of the people who were motivated by your marriage to wait on GOD. Anytime you find rebellion in yourself or your spouse, come against it; don't come against the spouse. Speak to the spouse about their position and pray with and for them so that they can get back in their places of obedience. Remember to bind up witchcraft anytime you see rebellion because the Bible tells us that rebellion is witchcraft.

4. You keep opposing her position, and she responds by opposing your position. Women are reflectors. Whatever you project, we will reflect. Sometimes, a woman doesn't reflect what you are doing out of retaliation; sometimes women do it as a response to your actions. Every communication starts when one person speaks, and the other person responds to what they said. Our actions also communicate with one another. The thing here is to stop opposing her position and just take your own.

5. You want to pursue your gifts the wrong way. This is the most common of them all. Sometimes, a man (or woman) will be truly gifted but want to pursue their gifts in the wrong way. For example, let's say that there is a man who has a wife and two children. He works for a local construction company and he barely makes enough money to support his growing family. An opportunity arises for him to go and play in a band in another state. He won't be getting paid for this gig, but it is a chance for him to get the exposure that he wants. To take this offer, his family would have to go hungry and depend on others to stand up. The wife opposes this, obviously because they have mouths to feed and bill collectors who all have mouths to feed. This is when priority has to come into play. Your first priority here is to provide for your family. If there is a way that you can continue feeding your family and providing their necessities, all the while pursuing your dreams, go for it. But, if a sacrifice has to be made; you should never opt to sacrifice your children's needs for your wants.

These are situations that actually do occur in marriage. Whatever the reason for the opposition, the fix is for you to get back in position and stop opposing GOD. When the two of you agree with GOD, you will never disagree with one another.

-Chapter 8-

<u>Fueling Her Design</u>

I remember that just before gas prices begin to
skyrocket, trucks had become the in-thing.
Everyone had to have an SUV or a pick-up truck.
Then, once gas prices went up and stabilized at $3
and higher, people started selling those trucks.
Many of them could not afford to pay for the fuel
for such a large vehicle, while others just didn't
want to pay that much for fuel. Whatever their
reasons were, they made a decision to get rid of
those vehicles, and the ones who decided to keep
them saw the positive side of having a large vehicle.

Your wife is similar to a vehicle. The larger the
vehicle, the more you are expected to put into it.
By larger, I mean the greater her anointing is. There
are some women who will never go past just being a
wife and a mother, and that in itself is a great
accomplishment. But, that's as far as they are
willing to go, so you won't have to put much into
them except what is expected of a husband. Then,
there are some women who were designed to do
much more. In addition to being a wife and a

mother, they are ministers and entrepreneurs. Such a woman has to be fueled for her destiny; therefore, she will require more, and anytime she doesn't reach her design's potential, she may break down. The same goes with a vehicle. If you put three dollars in gas in a vehicle and attempt to drive it to another state, that vehicle is likely to break down, and it won't run again until it gets more fuel. It has to have enough fuel to get it from where it is to where it's headed.

As her husband, you must understand her design and her potential. Then, you have to give her the tools and support that she needs to reach her design's potential. This means that you have to be a provider and a friend. You have to encourage her along the way and understand that her success is your success. She is designed to make you look great. Even when she fails, you must be there to pick her up and encourage her. When a woman fails a lot, it is not that she's doing the wrong thing; she just might be doing the right thing the wrong way. At that moment, she is simply trying to find her footing. As a husband, you should remain positive as she matures in her gifting. NEVER cause her to turn around from who she is because you're tired of her failing at being who she is. Don't be negative and don't ignore her. You need to fuel her design so that she can continue on. In the end, she is going to make you look great.

Think about a potted plant. In its pot, it can never reach its potential height. It has to adapt to its pot to survive. If that plant is removed from that pot and placed outside near a river, it will reach its maximum potential. Your wife is the same way. She is designed to reach a certain height, but if you are like a pot to her, she will adapt to you and never grow past a certain height. Instead of being her pot, be that open space that she needs near a river. Provide for her and watch her grow.

A lot of men complain that they can't afford their wives' expensive habits. Now, if she has a spending problem, you need to correct that. If she has an investing problem, you need to support her. Spending and investing are not the same. They are like plane tickets. Spending is a one-way ticket for your finances, and it basically says that wherever you are when your finances leave you, that's where you'll remain. Investing is like a two-way ticket. Whatever you send out is scheduled to return to you eventually, and it'll pick you up and take you to a better place. Spending is a minus sign that keeps on taking, but investing is a plus sign that keeps on adding.

When a woman is designed for greatness, she may invest a lot into who she is and what she wants. If she is investing in trying to be like her friends, then she is throwing away money and precious time. This is a trap that a lot of women fall into. Women often see their friends arriving at their blessed places, and they try to hijack their friends' planes. As a husband, you can correct this by reminding her of who she is and asking her to stay focused.

Your wife needs to be fueled according to her

design's potential. If you can't afford to fuel her financially, find a way to fuel her otherwise. In addition, you're never too old for growth. Most men are intimidated by a woman who has reached or is soaring towards her potential. If this is you, the error would be to try to prohibit her from reaching her full potential. The correct thing to do is to pray against pride, and if need be, stretch your limits and strive for greater.

Most men think they already know their wife's full potential, but this isn't true because even she doesn't know her full potential. GOD will reveal to her who she is layer by layer, as she obeys HIM and sheds her old ways. Thinking that you know how far she is called to go is error because once she reaches that place, you won't fuel her to go any further. Even if your wife failed out of school and she isn't what many would call "bright," that doesn't mean that she isn't wise. Man's intelligence comes from other humans. Some of the women of old were very wise, but they had no secular education. Never confuse artificial intelligence with wisdom because they are not one in the same. If you don't pot her in your understanding, she will grow to heights unimaginable.

One way to fuel her design is to learn to do some of the things that she will need. For example, if your wife has anointed hands, and she decided to go into gardening, it would be a great idea if you studied up on gardening so that you can be a support system to her. Women get charged up when their husbands join in and support what they are doing. All the same, women tend to lose interest in things that their husbands show no interest in. If what she does bores you, don't show it. There is something in what she does that you can learn to like. If she is a gardener, and you don't like to garden, you could study up on designing a lawn or building the fixtures that she'll need.

You may find that your wife jumps from one idea to the next, but this isn't something you should concern yourself with. Women are indecisive, and sometimes a woman will try several ideas before she settles down in one. You may discover that you liked her last idea, but you're not too fascinated with her new idea. In this case, continue to show support for both ideas. Don't fuel her up to chase the things that you want and refuse to support her in doing what she wants. That's like putting diesel in a car that requires unleaded gasoline. Your wife needs the right type of support, and she needs to be given this support consistently so that she doesn't run out of fuel and quit altogether.

There are a few men who are afraid to support their wives in what they do because they fear that their wives will arrive at the top, lose respect for them, and eventually leave them. So, to keep her from getting this big head and abandoning post, they intentionally discourage them and refuse to support them. When the wife does something that they feel won't make her this big shot that they fear, they support and encourage them. If this is your pattern of thinking, here are a few things that you should know:

1. A wife that loves her husband will never leave him once she has arrived in success. Oftentimes, if she is in submission to GOD, she will only lift you up as she goes along. She will encourage you to reach the top and she'll celebrate you when you do. Jean is a bio engineer, and he has studied in three countries, learned five languages, and he is a very accomplished man as far as achievements. Nevertheless, as I began to build, I saw success starting to come in my direction at an alarming rate. I was and am happy, but I am conscious about the fact that Jean is a husband who loves being able to provide for his wife. To him, this defines being a man. When I realized I was beginning to make more money than him, I didn't shun him. He didn't even really know at first because he never asks how much I made or what I'm doing with the money. Instead, he watches as I help with bills and offers to buy whatever is needed. I didn't rub it in his face or get puffed up. I decided to encourage him to go ahead and launch a few businesses where he is the main feature. Of course, everything that I own, he owns, because we are one person. I design for the most part, and he really doesn't have an interest to do what I'm doing because he wants to find his own way, but I encourage and support him.

2. Her blessing is your blessing. There was a time when I wasn't making a lot of money and Jean was trying to push me to get a job.

I fought hard because I didn't want to work in secular America. I knew what GOD had in store for me and I wanted to pursue my gifts. It really wasn't Jean's decision to let me sit at home and do what I'm doing; it was GOD'S. I'd prayed on it after getting lecture behind lecture from Jean, and GOD just opened up the windows of Heaven on me and silenced Jean. Since then, he's glad that he didn't try to force me out there because I'm able to do the work, keep the house clean, and have a hot meal waiting for him when he gets home. Not to mention I don't bring negativity from the workplace because I don't deal with negative customers. So I've had a great day almost every day!

3. It is always better to climb with your wife than it is to try to bring her down. You aren't her GOD, and you should never try to thwart GOD'S plans for her out of fear and selfishness. When you find yourself feeling discouraged or intimidated by the thought of your wife being successful, don't come against your wife, come against your fears. Always know where to direct your words and your feelings so that you don't launch an attack against a woman who desires to be a blessing to you.

4. Respond to your fears by fueling your faith. Anytime that fear comes over you, don't submit to it. Instead, go out and buy something to show your continued support for your wife. What you are doing is putting fear to shame by going against it and not

with it.

5.   Trying to stop her will only backfire. She is
      who she is, and you can't stop her from
      being such. If you try, GOD may have to
      remove you from her life so that she can
      reach her potential in HIM. You have to
      realize that it's not all about you and your
      feelings; it's about the Kingdom of GOD.
      Go for what GOD is for, and only go against
      what GOD is against; otherwise, in trying to
      challenge her, you will soon discover that
      you were, in reality, challenging GOD.

Just remember that no matter how blessed she is,
she is your wife and that makes you blessed along
with her. Fuel her design by being the provider that
she needs, offering up your support, and
encouraging her when she wants to quit. Believe
me; if she reaches her potential in CHRIST, she will
only make you look good!

Lastly, know how much fuel she needs and don't
give her any less or any more. To know this, you
have to ask GOD to teach you to cover such a
woman. Giving her too much fuel will only cause
her to become fearful of not being able to reach
your expectations of her. She's probably already
battling with the fact that she's called to such
greatness, but adding that extra fear on top will only
make her legs give from under her faith. Giving her
too little fuel will cause her to breakdown before
she arrives at her destination. Some men will place
a mental budget in their hearts and decide to support
their wives to a certain limit, but once they've gone

past this limit and not found success, these men will often turn on their wives and began to discourage them. One thing about her design is that it will produce its fruit in due season, not sooner. Sometimes we arrive at what looks like the doors of our breakthrough, only to find that they were more doors that led to more paths along our journey. The process that she is going through is for a reason and a season. Now, if you don't let her go through the process, she may find success and bolt like lightning because the process wasn't completed. The process is to continue to kill the flesh, remove the fears embedded in us, and to help us maintain our success when we've arrived in it. Sometimes people try to speed up the process, and they arrive at what they think is success, and then they are thrown all the way back to the bottom. They didn't appreciate the process, and the process was there to refine them and publish them as a new creature in CHRIST. The process is a continual renewing of our minds and a continual deliverance session. Don't rush the process and don't try to slow it down. Just let it play out season by season. And know that by success, I don't mean financial success; even though financial success is inevitable once one has successfully reached GOD'S potential for them. Success is to be in perfect alignment with GOD'S WORD and HIS will for you!

-Chapter 9-

Recovering From Adultery

Adultery is like working hard on a job for years and doing everything your boss says. You arrive at work early, and you leave work late. You tolerate things from your boss that no one else would tolerate, and then one day, you discover that when the time for promotion came, your boss chose someone else for the position. Even this example doesn't wholly describe the emotional toll that adultery puts on a spouse. It's devastating, and there are no words that can explain how traumatizing it is.

With that being said, the first thing you should know about adultery is that it is a crime of selfishness. It is as cold as the grave and as cruel as a heartless murderer. There are many ways in which the enemy could snuff your marriage out, but adultery is the cruelest one yet because it's like dying a slow death. I say that to discourage you from adultery or continuing in adultery. You need to know what it feels like and what it does to your spouse. In addition, your spouse needs to know what adultery does to you.

Your Spouse Committed Adultery
I know that it is an excruciating time for you, and there are no words that can release you from where you are today. The person that you love has betrayed you, and they didn't just do it once; it was a continuous affair, and now you're left to pick up the pieces. The decision of whether you should go or stay is plaguing you, but you need more time to think with a clearer mind. Nevertheless, the decision seems to be rushing you, and seeing your spouse in your mind's eye in submission to someone else is literal torment. Nevertheless, you haven't made your decision yet. Part of you wants to leave just to teach her a lesson. You know that the other man isn't going to stick with her, so the temptation is there to just let him have her. Then again, you've invested many years, blood, and sweat into the union, and it's not that easy just to get up and walk away.

What should you do? First and foremost, when adultery comes into the picture, another party needs to come in and intervene. You need to talk with your Pastor or a Christian Counselor that you know will mediate the matter. The reason for intervention is the person who was victimized by the adultery will likely not want to listen to the person who hurt them, and this is understandable. Don't be humiliated to share with your Pastor what you are going through. Now, if you know that your Pastor has loose lips, then of course you wouldn't talk to him or her. But, if you know that you were placed under their care by GOD; by all means, talk to him or her. Sometimes, they are able to get details out of the spouse that you can't get from them. Not the gruesome details of the affair, of course, but the details of why they felt the need to participate in an affair. When a woman has an affair, it is often in response to something; not necessarily something you did, but it can be a response to something on the inside of her. It may take several sessions for her to reveal the truth, and then again, she may decide to withhold the information out of fear or her desire to continue in the affair. Whatever she decides, you are not to lose yourself in your pain. Instead, make a decision and ask GOD to confirm or rebuke your decision.

It won't be easy, but don't keep pressing the spouse for details. Some people think that the details of the affair will ease the pain, but that's not true. It'll only give you a mental view and send you into a bout of rage that some like to call temporary insanity. Get to the root of the issue by speaking with your wife about her reasons for the affair. Maybe she did it in response to an affair that you had, or that she believes you had. Maybe she felt unloved and unappreciated by you. Maybe she's just a selfish woman who thinks the world ought to revolve around her. Nevertheless, your wanting to know why this affair took place should not be rooted in anything else but to help you start the healing process. Who knows? Maybe GOD will restore you, your wife and your marriage. Then again, maybe HE will separate the two of you so that you can seek answers from HIM without the distraction of having to see her and remember what she did every day.

What if the two of you decide to work through the matter? You decide to forgive her (which you have to do whether you leave or stay), and you want to work towards a better future for you and your family. How do you move through the pains associated with an affair? How do you erase the memories that haunt you? Please understand that we all heal at different paces. Therefore, your healing may take longer than others, or it may take less time than others. It's completely up to you. GOD has already instilled forgiveness in you, but pride makes us not want to tap into it. Most people think that if they forgive the person that the person won't learn their lesson. The truth is, you can't teach her or anyone a lesson; all you can do is pray for her and let GOD deal with her. Your focus should be on the restoration of your family, and more than that, helping your wife to be restored to CHRIST. You have to take the leadership role in your home, and call family meetings. Pray with your wife and read the Bible with her every day. While she is still growing, there will be days when she will want to rebel and not read the Bible. You can't force her, but what you can do is take the leadership role and read the Bible yourself. Keep praying about her, and GOD will change her slowly, but surely. Remember, the change is often slow, but it won't be unnoticeable. You will begin to see changes in her as the WORD begins to penetrate her.

In addition, plan more fun events with her. Some would say that giving your wife a good time is the same as rewarding her for her behavior, but it isn't true. If she's going to return to her sin, she'll do it whether you woo her or not. Your responsibility as a husband is not diminished by her actions, and again, you should NEVER take it upon yourself to punish the spouse. When you feel the pain welding up inside of you, rather than confronting her, go and confront the pain. Excuse yourself to another room and write her a letter. Once you're done, ball it up. What you're doing is letting the healing process run its course without adding contention and more heartache to it. If she knows why you are going into these states of mind, she may offer to come in and talk with you more about it. That part is up to you, but again, never ask for explicit details or you'll find that wound reopening again and again. If she doesn't offer to come in and comfort you during the mourning process, don't take offense. Some women don't know how to function on the wrong end of guilt, so they'll avoid any situation where they are deemed guilty.

Healing will take consistent prayer and a change of mind. You should choose a focal point in your future and work on achieving that. For example, if you decide that you want to move to Minnesota and start your own business, use that time to begin doing the necessary research and saving money. The key is to stay focused on GOD, and HE will focus on you and your situation. HE knows what it feels like to be cheated on because mankind is an unfaithful people. HE can relate to you, and HE can tell you what you need to do next. After all, HE is your designer, and HE knows how to fix you.

You Committed Adultery
In this case, your spouse will need to take the advice above, and you have to take a different position in the matter. One thing about an affair is that it is the worst kind of pain that a heart can bear. It's not just a betrayal, but it is a foundation-exposing event that will tear down everything you've ever built with your spouse. I tell people all the time that if they know that they have an adulterous heart to just let their spouses know and try to get healing from it. This is to stop you (the adulterer) from building a secure future for you and your family, only to have your secrets tear them down. It is not wise to invest in property or plan your future with someone when you know that you have fidelity issues. In doing so, you're basically saying that you believe that your wife will be with you despite your indiscretions. Many men are moved to violence when they find out otherwise. Can you imagine building a house with your sweat and hard work, only to have another man eventually call it home? Could you imagine saving up hundreds of thousands of dollars, only to have your wife take it in a divorce? Can you imagine visualizing a perfect future for you and your family, only to watch from afar as another man enjoys what you believe is rightfully yours? This is what happens when a person is investing their time and money into light and darkness. In the light, you have some wonderful things planned for you and your wife. In the dark, you are creating soul ties

with other women, and soul ties never fade away into the darkness; instead, they eventually come to the light.

But, let's say that it's already done. You committed adultery and your wife is devastated. You don't know what to do for her, and you don't know what is going to become of your marriage. What can you do?

First, the number-one thing that you should NOT do is play the victim. The worst thing that you can do is shift the blame to your spouse or try to get her to share in that blame, even if you truly believe that she pushed you to do it. No one can push you to have an affair, because adultery is a decision that first starts in the mind, makes its way to the heart, and then the body follows through with it.

Secondly, understand that everyone heals differently and at their own pace. Never think that your wife has had sufficient time to get over it, and that she's just parking there for fun. Give her the time that she needs to heal, but also ask her to go first into a room and write you a note when the hurt arises. Once she's done with that note, she can give it to you or throw it away. If she decides to hand it to you and the same questions are in the note that were in the previous one, answer her, but let her know that after three rounds the questioning has to stop. You want to start healing the union and not constantly revisit the sin itself; therefore, instead of talking about what was done, talk about what needs to be done to prevent this from happening again.

Buy her flowers and send her cards.

Thirdly, if you publicly humiliated her, you will have to publicly dignify her. A man once told me how he'd hurt his wife and how she'd left him. She refused to come back to him despite his efforts to reconcile. He admitted that he'd had an affair and that even her co-workers were aware of his affair. I told him what I'm about to tell you. Women love to be publicly doted on. When a woman receives flowers at work, she feels like a queen for a day. All of the women at work will gather around her and talk about how they wished their husbands (or boyfriends) would do the same for them. On the same note, any time a woman is publicly humiliated, her co-workers and others will gather to talk about her fall from grace. Sure, you may say that she shouldn't worry about what others are saying, but you have to be aware that this changes the environment at her job. She is made to be ostracized, and she is given pity instead of honor. She will feel like a walking plague going amongst people who know about her husband's affair. Therefore, you have to apologize publicly by sending her flowers with a note of apology, buying her gifts, coming to her job and taking her to break, and even saying aloud that you will do anything to win her back. Understand that adultery hurts on so many levels, but publicly redeeming yourself will help to soothe the humiliation part. You don't have to tell others what you've done (in case they don't know), but you should remove the humiliation from the equation. A great thing to do is to go to her job with 25 roses. If you can catch up with 10-25 of her co-workers, give each of them one rose to take to her and tell them to say to her that you said you are sorry for upsetting her and that you are sending this rose as a token of your love for her. Again, you don't have to say what was done; just show her that you are sorry.

Next, remember that the imagination is a place where dreams take place, but it also a place where nightmares flourish. Sometimes, your wife will revisit those pains in her mind. What you should do is occupy her mind with positive things so that the negative things won't keep coming to visit her. Too much idle time will give her ample opportunity to dwell on what was done and send her into an emotional spiral. Take her out more and continue this behavior over the course of her life.

Lastly, and more importantly, do not lie about your affair or affairs. An affair is layers and layers of lies, and you want to remove these lies from your marriage. Adding another lie to the layer won't help her to heal, but it'll keep her digging for the truth. Believe me, she will find the raw truth, and she won't be prepared for it. Women have built-in investigative capabilities that would put to shame even the best private eye. If she endured an affair, she's strong enough to hear the truth. Once the whole truth is out in the light, she can begin the healing process, but if you are still withholding information, she hasn't even begun the process yet. If she asks you how the affair started, tell her the truth. If she asks you how many times you had sex with the woman, tell her the truth. If she asks you if you wore protection, tell her the truth.

Acknowledge your guilt and humble yourself. In this, the other woman (or women) won't be able to come back and tell her something that you haven't already told her. You can ask her not to ask about explicit details, and you shouldn't give explicit details of the sex itself. That can be traumatizing to anyone. But, women often ask the following questions:

Why?

What did I do wrong that made you feel the need to seek for sex outside of me?

How many times did you sleep with her?

Was she worth it?

Why didn't your conscious kick in?

If you were sorry or felt guilty, why did you keep going back for more?

So, I'm not good enough for you?

You're not attracted to me anymore?

You may even find your wife changing her look and her behavior. Help her to find her way back to herself. She has been torn down, and she feels the need to rebuild herself as a different woman so that she won't endure the heartache of another affair. Again, remember the pain is great, and you can't discount it just because you don't feel it.

The both of you should love and respect one another enough to remain faithful. More than that, you need to both learn to be faithful to GOD. In doing so, you will automatically learn to be faithful to one another.

From today, start a whole new foundation in CHRIST and begin building from there. Recommit yourself to CHRIST and to one another. Be sure to follow through and be honest with one another. If an affair took place, the offending spouse should be willing to do whatever is necessary to save their marriage. This includes changing their phone numbers. If the person that you committed adultery with came to your job, or found another way to contact you, tell your spouse each time. This is how you show your spouse that you are committed to the relationship and that this person is a history lesson. And if your spouse is the offending spouse, she should do the same.

Love never fails, but it is tried. Love isn't selfish or boastful. It is humble, and its arms stretch outside of our understanding to embrace us and all that we are in CHRIST JESUS. Love your spouse beyond their faults, and be just as lovable as you want them to be.

-CHAPTER 10-

Bedroom Blues: The Infamous 'No'

How many times has a married woman come to me and talked about her husband complaining about her being tired, having a headache, or just not wanting to sleep? He wants to minister to her in the bedroom, and she doesn't want his ministry. As a husband, the infamous "no" represents so many negative things. It says that she is not happy with him in the bedroom, she's no longer in love with him, or she is possibly having an affair. For a wife, however, oftentimes, it's just a "no." All the same, when a wife constantly says "no," it can be a signal that something is wrong in the marriage. She may not see it initially, but a woman's body responds to how she feels.

For example, an argument breaks out about an ongoing issue. The husband goes to his wife and apologizes about the way he reacted and the things he said. He wants to seal the apology with some lovemaking. Now, as a husband, you probably wouldn't see why she would say "no," but any wife reading the book will get stuck at the words "ongoing issue." That means the problem is one that has not been resolved. Therefore, the sun will go down on her anger. Again, remember, men are projectors and women are receptors. Men often project the issue onto the wife, and women store the issue until it's ready to be born. Imagine if she's full of several ongoing issues. Now, because the husband isn't carrying the issue, he can forget about it and want to move forward, but for a wife, the issue needs to be settled and put to rest.

It's not a bad thing in her or in you; the problem is, you have to understand one another's design and act accordingly. Understand that your wife stores issues, and she has to understand that you don't store them.

In addition, you should know that women aren't often stimulated by physical activity; they are stimulated by mental activity. Therefore, trying to sleep with your wife without first stimulating her mind will often be met by a "no." She's not saying that she isn't physically attracted to you; she is basically saying that her mind has not given her body a "yes" because her mind has something else going on.

How do you remedy this issue and get your wife to want to sleep with you? By romancing her mind and not her body. Again, you must understand the design of a woman. Know that in everything we do, we are either a beginner, intermediate, or a professional. A lot of women will say that their husbands are still beginners or at the intermediate level in the bedroom, but very few women say that their husbands are professionals. Your goal is to not get to one level and stay there. You should study your wife like you're preparing for a huge test (because you are), and then do everything in your power to pass the test. How do you do this? Here are a few tips that will surely help you out.

1. Make sure that there are NO unresolved issues in your marriage. Unresolved issues take a toll on the wife the most because she is a carrier. Remove that weight from her, and you'll get a better response.

2. Compliment her a lot and show her that you are still smitten by her. Oftentimes, we as spouses get comfortable with one another and forget to woo one another. When you start acting like a brother, she'll respond to you like a sister. That means there will be no sex, but plenty of words. But, when you start acting like a husband, she'll respond as a wife. Be random and non-predictable. Don't sound sarcastic or monotone. Look her in the eyes and just compliment her.

3. Romance her often. Women know what comes at the end of a romantic encounter with their husbands. Take her out, buy her gifts, and show that you appreciate spending time with her. Don't just jump in the bed smelling like outdoors and Old Spice.

4. When you take a woman out, don't EVER EVER complain about how much you're spending or have spent. Women like to live in the moment, but when you start to focus on the negatives, she'll store that negative

energy.

5. If she is stressed about something, try to help her out with the issue. Because men are projectors, they often hate to have problems placed on their laps. Instead, encourage her and the both of you take the issue to CHRIST. If a woman is weighed down by something, she will not want to add your weight on her.

6. We're all grown (hopefully), so here goes. Make sure you're not the only one getting pleasure in the bedroom. I know you may be getting older and everything seems to either speed up or slow down. But you are in control of your body and your mind. Never make a lovemaking session all about you.

7. Take care of her design. Give her what she needs. For example, let's say that your wife is gifted and she wants to create and sell gift baskets. You complain about the economy and say no to her. She comes back another day and says that she is thinking about writing a book, but again, you either say or show your disapproval for her new decision. Understand that every woman has something in her that has to be birthed. Always support who she is in GOD.

8. Help her with her workload. Sometimes women overwork themselves and can feel overwhelmed. Take some of that work upon yourself and also delegate some of it to the children, if you have any that are old enough to take on the responsibilities. Letting a

wife cook, clean, help the children with homework, clean up some more and work an eight-hour job...and then expecting sex all the time is a definite no for most women. Her body is worn out from the work, and her mind is exhausted. Help her out, and she'll help you out.

9. Don't be perverted with it. Again, sex is mental for a woman, not just physical. If you're running in the bedroom with tools, chainsaws, and all kinds of gadgets; she will likely be turned off. Why? Because to a woman, you are basically saying that you don't know how to please her, or that you are twisted. You don't need all of those gadgets when your marriage is in right-standing with GOD. Know this: If a battery isn't charging up on its own, there will come a time when even the spark plugs won't get it to start. Learn how to please your wife naturally. GOD gave both of you the tools to please one another. You can please one another more than most people that are perverted and bring all kinds of gadgets into the bedroom. They are trying to get the power that can only be found in a GODLY marriage. You're in a GODLY marriage hopefully, so you don't need to bring man-made objects into the bedroom when you are GOD-made.

10. Remain faithful. With women, an affair takes the specialness out of sex. When a woman is married, she feels special because she knows that she is the only woman who

gets to enjoy the man that she has. But, when that man goes off and gives himself over to another woman, the wife no longer feels special; she feels used. Read the section about adultery so that the both of you can get past it.

11. You're not taking the lead. Even in the animal kingdom, the dominant male gets the girls. If your response is always, "Whatever you want. I don't care. Yes, dear," you are painting yourself in a bad light. While women do want their husbands to listen to them and give them the freedom to do things, women also enjoy a husband who takes the lead and makes decisions.

12. You're too selfish. If selfishness is disgusting to GOD, imagine how it looks to your wife. Spend your time being selfless, and she should do the same for you. It is then that you will see a better response.

13. Keep the atmosphere positive. There is no worse place to be than in a bad atmosphere with a horny man. There are many things that will ruin the weather in your home or marriage. Maybe it's the people that visit you or the music that you listen to. Everything and everyone that comes into your home, comes into your marriage and will set the atmosphere for your marriage. If someone comes to your house and always thickens the atmosphere, you need to pull that welcome rug from under them. If something in your home is messing with the atmosphere in the wrong kind of way, put it

out of your home.

14. Lastly, she has to understand that as your wife, she is to submit her body to you and vice versa. But she may not know this; therefore, make sure she is getting WORD-fed often. Don't use the Bible to try to get her to submit, however. Talk to her and let her know how you feel. Ask her how she feels and ask for the truth. Ask her what she feels that you can do differently or what she doesn't like. Don't just assume that she likes something, because you'll end up turning your wife off instead of turning her on.

15. Her pain isn't always her pleasure. Learn her body and learn what she responds to and what she does not respond to. I have literally heard men joke about how well they take care of business in the bedroom and seen their wives give the back of their heads that oh-so-unmistakable eye. Please remember...just because it's good to you, doesn't mean it's good to her. Learn what pleases her. One thing that you'll find is that GOD created everything to work at its best in unity. If she concentrates on pleasing you, and you concentrate on pleasing her, you will have a sex life that legends are made of. But anytime one person gets selfish, it ruins the experience for the next person.

CHAPTER 11

Silencing a Roaring Engine

A complaining and angry woman is not on any man's wish list; nevertheless, most men don't know that the women they are courting can be mouthy until they've married them. Constant bickering has ruined many marriages, and with women, we sometimes don't know when to close our mouths and open our ears. Most women are naturally talkative. If you find us on the phone with one another, you will often see that women can go on and on about absolutely nothing for hours on end. Add to the fact that women are emotional creatures, and you've got a talkative woman who is hell bent on fixing what she sees as a dent in her marriage.

Women look for forgiveness in words, but men look for forgiveness in silence. How do you bring these two creatures together without incident? Let's use a car as an example. You have a car that you drive around, and you've learned to do what it takes to keep that car running. You keep the fluids checked, the tires balanced, and regular maintenance on the vehicle. When you neglect the vehicle, after a while, the vehicle's engine starts to roar. Occasionally, old parts have to be replaced for the car to run silently. For example, most men know when the muffler has to be changed because of the loud noise that comes from the engine. Sure, it's no fun having to go and pay someone to fix your car, but you do it because you need your car.

Think of your wife in the same way. She needs to be checked, her mind needs to be balanced, and she requires regular maintenance. Anytime something is being neglected, you will hear her roar. I tell men all the time that the easiest thing to do is quiet a quarreling woman. It's easier to quiet her than it is to quiet a neglected car.

What should you do? First, take notes of her complaints and compile them for a month or so. Put them somewhere you know she won't find them. The best place I can suggest is to write them in a document, save the document and upload it as private to a document hosting site. Use a password that you don't ordinarily use and delete the document from your computer. Date the document and jot down the complaint. List what happened initially that started the complaint, and list her mood for that day. What you are doing is studying your wife. After you've found what you see to be as her trigger point, print off all the documents and call a family meeting. You're the head of the home, so you have to nip this behavior in the bud. As a husband and a leader, you have an advantage over your wife. That advantage is you are not controlled by your emotions, and this makes you the stronger creature. That's why GOD gave you the lead position. Call this meeting on a happy day when your wife is in an okay or good mood. It is even a great idea to ask someone in your family to keep your children that day, or conduct this meeting after the children have went to bed. Pull out two folders with the same documents in them. Each document should contain journal like entries of the days that she was acting contentious, and the things that triggered her that day. List her overreactions and how you felt when she was acting that way. Then lay out the law in your home. Tell her that you are the husband and the head and that you love her, but this behavior has got to stop. She has to find a better way of communicating with you that doesn't involve yelling, sarcasm, crying, or any negative behavior. You don't tell her that you are going to do something drastic if she doesn't listen, but you tell her that the behavior has to stop, and it has to stop that particular day. Ask her to list all of her problems in the marriage on the back of the papers that she was handed so that you can rectify them today. Tell her that you are willing to listen to her intently, but you want a new law set in place when that meeting is over. Believe it or not, most women won't find this behavior offensive, because women love when their husbands take the lead to protect them and their marriages. Now, if she's a contentious woman who believes that she is just as much man as you are, a lot more is going to be needed.

Some of the mouthiest women are capable of being some of the most submissive women. Their heads just need to be covered. Who are their heads? You are. *"But I would have you know, that the head of every man is Christ; and the head of the woman is the man; and the head of Christ is God" (1 Corinthians 11:3).* You have to be covered by the CHRIST, which means that you are to be in subjection to HIM. When a wife knows that she can trust her husband's lead, she is more likely to quiet down. When women see that their husbands are being led by their flesh or the flesh of others, they won't trust the leads of these men, and understandably so. Submission isn't just one person submitting to the other; proper submission is order, and it is everyone in submission to their head until the head covering them is JEHOVAH. Men that usually demand to be heads are oftentimes fleshly and don't understand what it means to be the head, but a man who understands his position and his role often doesn't demand his position, he takes it. Being the head is not dominating the wife; being the head is leading the wife and also trusting the wife in her role as a helpmate. That means to understand that the wife is wrong sometimes, and you are wrong sometimes. A wise man learns to listen to his wife's advice, AND THEN he takes it to his head (CHRIST) and does with it whatever the LORD says to do with it. When Sarah told Abraham to put Hagar and Ishmael out, Abraham didn't want to listen. The Bible says that her request grieved him. GOD then told Abraham to hearken (listen) to his wife. In this, Abraham was doing as GOD said, not as Sarah said.

But, what if you have one of those wives who truly

wants a position of power over you? What can you do? Stay in position and refuse to submit to her rule, because it is out of order for her to dominate you. If her head is uncovered, she will pick up all manners of witchcraft, and you don't want that mess in your home. Rebellion is witchcraft, and if your home is not lined up in the right order, your home is covered by witchcraft.

Remember maintenance. Sometimes women become depressed when they are doing the same things over and over again. They want to try something new. Never in your life get to the point where you are not doing something fun with your wife. Take her out, and the both of you should have a great time. Wives like to be courted continuously; the courtship doesn't end after the nuptials. Take her out often, cook for her sometimes, and be sure to service her as a husband often. Buy her cards, write her notes, tell her that you love her daily, kiss her often, compliment her a lot, and help her when she needs help. If she says to you that a particular woman likes you, believe her and act accordingly. Women can see what you can't, just like men can see what we can't. If she says to you that one of your friends isn't good, believe her and act accordingly. As a wife, I have to tell you that I have NEVER said one of my husband's friends was bad and been wrong about it. NEVER. Now, if she has motive to not like him, then definitely pray about it and be sure that she is wrong before you address the matter. If she says that she doesn't like a particular family member of yours coming to her house, listen to her and act accordingly. Again, if she has motive as to why she is saying this, pray about it and address the matter once GOD has given you an answer. What you are doing is looking for ways to maintain peace in your home. You won't change her mind, but you can change the atmosphere of your marriage by not contending with her. All the same, she must respect your lead and honor you in the same way. One of the worst things that one can do to a spouse is to tell them to do something that they themselves refuse to do.

Remember the muffler. When the muffler gets old, it has to be replaced. Your wife isn't a muffler, of course, but her attitude is. When you begin to see a negative shift in her attitude, her heart needs a good cleaning out. Again, call a meeting and tell her to replace that attitude.

Remember to check her fluids. Her fluids are any and everything that is running through her life. For example, if you notice that she has been different in the wrong kind of way since she started hanging with a particular woman, talk to her about it. You have the right to say that you don't want her around this woman, and that the woman is not welcome in your home. If she is a woman of GOD who is in submission to the GOD in you, she will listen. If she's rebellious, she will rebel, and in that case, you should take your position and refuse to stand down. Pray to your head about her and stand in as her head. You are acting as her protector. Now, if you just don't like the friend because she's been spending too much time with her, don't do this. The only time that you should request that your wife stop hanging with a particular person is when GOD tells you that the person isn't good. HE may speak to you through your discernment, or HE may show you some things. Listen to your head and act accordingly.

Other fluids include family members, music, and so on. Everything that communicates with us is pouring its contents into us. We are like cups that are constantly being filled. If we're not being filled with wisdom, we are being filled with foolishness. That's the reality of it all. Don't try to dominate your wife, because that's not acting as a head. A head turns the body by making a decision and heading in the way that it has decided to go. The body has no choice but to follow.

Remember the tires. Your wife's pride will often inflate and deflate. You will see this over the course of your marriage. Some days, she may be happy and full of the love of GOD; other days, she may be contentious, boastful, or a little too low. When she is feeling down and out, fill her with the right things. Encourage her by telling her that she is beautiful and deserving of the best. Vow to protect her against anything that is attacking her. Listen to her so that she can pour out all the wrong things, and when she is emptied, fill her with the right things. When a wife sees that you are acting as her husband and best friend, she can relax and take her place as a wife.

Now, when she's being contentious or boastful, you aren't to deflate her; you have to deflate that lying pride. How do you do this? By taking your position as the head of the home. Talk to her about her mannerisms and tell her the truth. Let's say that she became intimidated because the two of you were out at the supermarket, and one of your ex-girlfriends was there. The ex-girlfriend passed you by and spoke to you, but didn't speak to your wife. As a husband, of course, you should observe this behavior and act accordingly. If she doesn't address your wife, don't you address her. Anyhow, your wife is now fuming because of this, and she won't let the incident go. When you arrive home, she goes on to talk about how she is so much prettier than your ex, and how she is classier. She is filling herself with hot air in order to feel superior to what she sees as her competitor. Instead of going along with this, build up your wife in the right way, but deflate all of that foolishness that's romancing her mind. Tell her that it's not about who is prettiest, classiest, or the best lover. Remind her that you chose to marry her, and that she should never be intimidated in her role as a wife. Be honest with her and let her know that her insecurities are bothering you because you know that you love her, and there is no other woman in this world but her designed just for you. Come up with an action plan. Say, for example that the next time you come into a situation like this, the both of you will greet her simultaneously and keep walking. You are offering to stand on her side, and this will make her feel better. But, again...if she feels threatened in her place, you need to secure her so she won't be so shaky. You'd do that for the door if it started squeaking, right? Do that for your wife. Secure her by talking to her and telling her what she needs to hear and telling her what you don't want to hear. Never come off as defending another woman, because that can start a fire of an argument, but let your angle be to build your wife up and tear down her pride. There is no need to tear down the other woman.

Always remember to take proper care of your wife. Give her what she needs, and she will give you more. Women are carriers. We are designed to take what you give us and give birth to something greater or something worse. It all depends on what you give us.

-Chapter 12-

<u>Legalizing an Illegal Union</u>

Let's face it. Many Christians marry the wrong person, whether the person is a believer or not. Satan likes to catch us when we are still babes in CHRIST and are wowed by the slightest of gestures. It's like the reaction you get out of a one-year-old when you take her in front of a mirror for the first time. She's moved by what she sees, and she's fascinated by what she sees. After a while, her reflection doesn't fascinate her anymore. Over the years, she may become horrified at what she sees if she doesn't take proper care of herself.

Marriage works the same way. Courting and marriage aren't the best of friends because courting often lies to marriage and promises that the person in question is the perfect candidate for you. Then, you get married and find out that not only did courting lie, but courting fled shortly after the wedding. When we are young in CHRIST, we are amused by just about anything. A woman who has never had the door opened for her may overreact when someone opens a door for her for the first time. I remember hearing a woman get loud and brag about a man spending $30 on her for lunch. I was surprised because she was over 40-years-old, and here she was, having never been treated out to dinner. She was to-the-moon with joy and concluded that he was a great man. I've seen men overreact about the slightest of gestures as well. I've heard men brag about women bringing them lunch to their jobs, and they said that this little gesture was enough to show them that these women were the one. Now, of course, after a few years into the union, they are singing a different tune, because there is a difference between a woman doing the right thing and a wife doing what comes naturally to her. We often marry the people that appeal to who we are at the moment and what they do for us at that moment. Oftentimes we, as human beings, go into relationships with the wrong kind of people over and over again. We become attracted to a certain kind of person, and when one person comes along on that level and does something different than our previous love interests, we think we've hit the jackpot. What people have to realize is that when you start seeing a change in the partners you choose for yourself, it often reflects a change is being made in us. But, it doesn't mean that you are necessarily ready for marriage at that moment. It just means that a change is happening and you need to wait for GOD to finish the work in you and call you a husband before you become a married man.

What if you married the wrong spouse? Can you just divorce her and go and remarry the right one? No. Once you take on the role of a spouse, you take on the responsibilities of a spouse. Your job is made harder because you chose the wrong person to fill the wrong position in your life, and she did the same thing...so, her job is no picnic as well. The both of you need to come to terms with the fact that you disobeyed GOD and now you have to find a way to make things right with HIM. After you have repented, you should ask HIM to rewire your wife to be your helpmate. Why does she need to be rewired and not you? Men were given the role as the head of the house, and as such, the blueprints for their assignments were given to them. The wife, however, was called to be a helpmate. Of course, she has her anointing and her callings, so she has purpose as well. This won't be taken from her, but to be rewired is to ask GOD to instill in her what she needs to be your helpmate and join you on the journey HE has given you. In the same, ask HIM to give you what you need to fuel her design and to cover here wherever she is called to be.

Understand that if GOD didn't call it together, Satan called it together because the foundation of your marriage was disobedience. The foundation of disobedience has to be torn down, and everything that was put into the union initially has to be uprooted. This means that you have to start the building process all over again in CHRIST. No, this isn't fun, but it is necessary. Oftentimes, we don't want to tear down the very things that we've come to love, but would you rather keep building on a shaky foundation and have it fall down once you've got comfortable in it, or would you rather start over and build it right?

Think about due process. According to Wikipedia, due process is: "the legal requirement that the state must respect all of the legal rights that are owed to a person. Due process balances the power of law of the land and protects the individual person from it. When a government harms a person without following the exact course of the law, this constitutes a due-process violation, which offends against the rule of law." Due means that something is owed to that person, and of course, process means a systematic occurrence purposed in creating, defining, or destroying something. Before that woman became your wife, there was something owed to her. Because of who she is, her build came with certain parts missing that only her husband could give to her. When she doesn't receive what is due to her, she will feel violated because a void will form in her. Whatever it is that she is missing, she needs it to continue on in her design. After all, this is owed to her, and she must collect it. Of course, if you weren't anointed to be her husband, but you married her out of rebellion, you don't have what she needs to complete her for the journey. You have man parts, but that's it. She needs more. Her design required that she go through a process, and this process was to equip her and qualify her for whatever GOD has in store for her. She didn't complete the process because she stopped it when she married the wrong man. You, on the other hand, are a giver. You were given what you need, and you were called to impart what was given to you to your wife. That's why men are imparters or givers of life, and women are receptors who birth life.

Women who aren't given what they need to go further often go into depression. They feel that there is something that they need, but they don't know what it is. They will indulge in all types of new activities trying to find their missing part. They will talk to some of the shadiest characters trying to find answers about the location of their missing part. They don't know that they married the wrong man. What they know is that they aren't birthing what they feel they were supposed to be birthing.

To fix this, again, you have to go before the LORD and repent. When David took Uriah's wife and had Uriah killed, he had to be punished, and the punishment didn't just end with the death of their firstborn. The punishment continued on generation to generation. Amnon ended up raping his sister Tamar; Absalom eventually killed Amnon to avenge his sister, and Absalom tried to kill his father to take his position as king. As you can see, disobedience sets off a network of wrongs that sometimes continues for years. Now, GOD has promised us that every man is accountable for his own sin. So, your children are no longer punished for your actions, but the punishment still stays with you for years on end. This means that you may endure years of watching your wife go through changes, and you go through changes so that the both of you can be right for one another. But, GOD will give you the strength that you need to get through those years. Remember, David had to repent of his sin and accept the punishment.

I can truly say that both times that I got married, it was out of rebellion. I got married because I wanted to be married, and the man before me at the time was everything I thought I wanted. I didn't know I was called to grow up in CHRIST, and that my needs would change over time. After the end of my first marriage, I quickly jumped into another marriage. I was so used to being a wife that I didn't want to go back to being anyone's girlfriend. So, when I met a man who was different, I was sold. I was going through a divorce and dating my now husband. This was absolute sin! It was wrong, and I had to be punished for it. Trust me; we went through some of the most excruciating years initially. It was no easy task to learn to be his wife, and I'm sure he'd say the same thing about me. I planned divorce many times. I called lawyers, looked for ways to get back to my hometown, and I asked my husband again and again for a divorce. I was still a woman trying to adapt to being a wife, and he was still a man trying to adapt to being a husband. Add our cultural differences on top of that, and you've got one big mess. Add the fact that we were unequally yoked, and you've got a recipe for disaster. So, again, I thought about divorce a lot. I actually dreamed about it, prayed for it, and threw fits because I wanted it. My husband would always tell me that he didn't believe in divorce and we'd just work it out, but my thoughts were, how can we work out being unequally yoked? Finally, I stopped thinking that I was the victim, and I accepted my role in the mess that we'd created. I had married the man, and I needed to learn how to be his wife.

GOD began ministering to me about my ways, and I submitted myself to change. Truthfully, it didn't take a very long time for the change to take place because I was willing to accept the change. I stopped crying and throwing fits, and I started listening to my husband. I started praying for my husband and encouraging him. I stopped trying to attack the man that he was, and I started respecting who he would become. I began ministering to him through my life, and I accepted that I would have to watch him grow up in CHRIST. It wouldn't be a pretty scene; I knew that because it wasn't a pretty scene when I was growing up. Then, he had to watch me grow up in CHRIST and mature in CHRIST. That transformation wasn't glamorous at all. Actually, it was hideous because my flesh had to die, and it did not die without a fight.

Nowadays, I humbly accept my role, and my build has been changed to fit the husband I have. All the same, he has changed a lot and continues to grow closer to GOD each day. He only learned to lead when he learned to be led by CHRIST. I couldn't lead him, so I stopped trying to. In the same, I learned that I could have possibly been the right wife for him. I just met him in the wrong season of both of our lives. We are truly at peace now, and we don't argue anymore. Occasionally, we may use a tone with one another, but we both quickly humble ourselves and listen to one another's point of view. This means the contention went out when he stopped contending with who he was in CHRIST, and I stopped contending with him. He has learned to respect and fuel my design, and I have learned to be his helpmate, but only through CHRIST JESUS. None of this happened overnight. It was a process that almost took us out, but we survived because we chose to pray, and because we chose to obey what GOD told us.

Your marriage can work; you've just got to be willing to do the work.

-CHAPTER 13-

A Better Neighborhood of Thinking

When a woman gets married, she often hopes that her new husband will move her into a better neighborhood. If she's in a bad neighborhood, she wants to be moved to a good neighborhood. If she is in a good neighborhood, she wants to be moved to a better neighborhood. Either way, women expect to see a change in their situation when they get married.

When a man gets married, he often expects to stay in the neighborhood that he's in. Men generally get comfortable in a place and see no need to move away. But the truth is, a husband is supposed to come into the union as a covering, a protector, a provider, and a builder. Therefore, it is not wrong for the wife to expect to be moved into a better place.

The differences between men and women aren't there to divide us; they are present to help us complement one another. We often expect to fit well with one another, when in truth, GOD designs us to fit into HIM. In doing so, we automatically fit well with our spouses. As human beings, however, we often shift from the highs and lows of living, and we expect our spouses to meet us where we are and relate to us there. When they don't, contention follows, and we declare that our spouses are bad. This isn't true. Anytime we feel a shift in our lives, we need to make sure we are secured in the WORD of GOD. The problem with many spouses is that we often expect one another to bear some of our growing pains, when we can't. When a wife has a baby, her husband doesn't share in the pain. Instead, he should be there to support and encourage her while she is in delivery. In addition, he should be there to provide, protect, and shelter her as she carries his child. When his wife has a situation that is hurting her, he should do the same. If he can get into that situation and take the brunt of the pain, he can if GOD allows him. But, of course, this should be prayed about, because sometimes GOD allows the pain to come to teach that person a valuable and life-saving message. In other words, don't run in front of GOD'S rod of discipline and take your wife's licks. If they are for her, she is designed to survive them and learn from them. Now, if it is an attack from the evil one, you are to go in and battle on your wife's behalf. You need to pray and understand what is happening before you run into the situation.

When we get married, we (women) also expect our husbands to move us into a better neighborhood of thinking. Women want to learn from their husbands, and women want people to see a positive change in their lives that their husbands have brought into it. Now, your wife should already be in a righteous neighborhood of thinking when you meet her. She should be a believer and as such, she should be in a place of wholeness. At the same time, you should be a believer in a place of wholeness. In being whole, you are not expected to complete one another; you are expected to complement one another. There is a difference. Two broken people make one complete mess.

How do you move her into a better neighborhood of thinking when she's already supposed to be there? By teaching her what she does not know. Understand that we are never at the full knowledge of GOD, but the husband is the head, and he should always be a knowledgeable head. In this, the wife should always be able to come to the husband to ask a question about the WORD. If you don't know, you should be directly under the Head (CHRIST), and as such, you will be able to provide an answer to her after you ask HIM. Your wife should not have to come in and guide you, for this is out of order. Because CHRIST is our head, we are known as the body of CHRIST. As the head of the wife, she is known as the body of the man. Could you imagine a body going in one direction and the head trying to go in another direction? A house divided against itself cannot stand, and every kingdom divided against itself is bought to desolation. *(See Matthew 12:25)* This means that you have to become one in your ways. GOD already called you one when you married one another, but now you must act as one person. Sure, you will have a difference in opinion quite often, but opinion should always submit to the WORD of GOD.

To move your wife into a better neighborhood doesn't mean that you teach her what you know today and keep her there forever. The both of you need to continually learn more about your FATHER which art in Heaven. You should always seek wisdom, knowledge and understanding. You should always be a provider for your wife; not just with the things, but even more with the wisdom, knowledge and understanding that she'll need to fuel her design. Court wisdom and dine at her table often. This is one affair your wife wouldn't mind you having, because wisdom will shower you with so much knowledge, understanding, and the things that the both of you want. Wisdom is the principal thing, so seek wisdom every day. A man that can continually teach his wife is a man who will always find peace in his home. If we aren't learning something, we are forgetting something. If we're not adding to us, we are subtracting from us. We are creatures created to be fed and grow. We need the bread of life continually, and if you starve your family of the bread of life, you will see them begin to turn on one another. Wisdom is needed to get you through this thing we call life, and to get you through it safely. Wisdom is needed to protect your family and guard them against the attacks of the enemy. Wisdom is needed to provide for your family because your flesh can fail you, but wisdom will never fail you. Wisdom is needed to lead your wife and your family because there are many paths set before you, but how do you know which one you are to take? Wisdom will always shed a light on the path that she has carved out for you. Wisdom is needed to guide you with your decisions because we don't know how to make rightful decisions on our own. Instead, we are creatures of adaption, and we often take the routes that are familiar to us because we've adapted to those routes. This means that we take the same routes over and over again, but wisdom will take you in a whole new and unfamiliar direction. In getting wisdom, you are operating as river that's attached to the Almighty GOD, and you will provide a continuous flow of blessings to your family. With wisdom, you will know something is wrong before wrong even tries to enter your home. You'll be able to prepare for this attempted intrusion, meet the enemy on his journey there, and send him back running. With wisdom, you won't just be the man, but you will be a man after GOD'S own heart. If you know how valuable wisdom is, you'll understand why so many families are being divided. If you know how valuable wisdom is, you'll seek her every day, because wisdom gives gifts every day to those that embrace her.

To bring your wife into a better neighborhood of thinking, you have to be constantly moving. You can't just stand still where you are and get comfortable there. The enemy is always trailing someone, but when you are in CHRIST, he can never catch up to you. When you stop in a certain place and start unpacking your life there, the enemy will catch up to you and try to take you out and take your family out. You are like the earth; you must be on the move constantly to sustain life. You can't stop, and you can't become complacent. You have to keep going forward and learn not to be afraid of the steps ahead of you. Success doesn't bite, and failure won't kill you, but failure is that tough professor that is so hard on you that you pass his class so that you never have to return to it. Fear opposes faith, so don't be led by fear because in doing so, you are allowing fear to become your head. No woman wants a fearful man. Only fear GOD.

We talk about the wife's design, but here's something about your design that you need to know. You were designed to keep on moving forward and advancing as a soldier of GOD. You were not designed for failure, and fear is the wrong kind of fuel for you. It'll break you down every time. You were not designed to get comfortable in any certain place, but you were designed to continually search out the heart of GOD. As you move forward in HIM, your family is blessed day after day. In every neighborhood that you go into, you are always ready to move to something better because you know the knowledge of GOD has no ends, and the wisdom of GOD is infinite. Even when the enemy attacks you where you are, you are to advance against him and keep pressing forward in CHRIST. In your obedience, you will cause the enemy to flee, and your family will be able to loot whatever the enemy left in his haste to get away from you.

Move your family forward every day. Ask yourself

every day, "What have I learned that will benefit my family today? What knowledge have I fed my family today?" Even if it is to learn one scripture, you have done exceedingly well because you are giving them something that will benefit them over the course of their life. Of course, with a scripture, you will need to explain it and ask questions.

Never be willing to settle into a place just because it's different from the place you've just left. There is better before you; you just need to go forth and take what is yours.

Kick pride out of your marriage, for pride is the enemy's way of dividing your marriage. There is so much power in unity, and this power renders the enemy powerless; therefore, he appeals to a man's (or woman's) selfish nature to get them to divide against one another. Don't let him do this in your house. Come together in unity with your family against the devil and watch him flee your presence faster than he entered it.

If you see that your wife has selfish ways, don't attack her; come against the pride of the issue. Remember, in the animal kingdom, a pride is a group of lions. If you attack one, you must fight and kill them all. The same thing goes with the pride of man. It doesn't come alone; it's often guarding foolishness, rebellion, unforgiveness, and envy. So, to get rid of this pride, you must attack everything that is a part of that pride. Pray against it and attack it with knowledge each day. Every time knowledge enters a person <u>and is received</u>, foolishness is evicted from that person. Slowly, as time goes on, that person will become wiser and change will be inevitable.

Your wife should see a change in her life for the better (and vice versa) once you enter it. You should always be prepared to move her into a new place in her mind, and this means that you are always moving into a new way of thinking yourself. In your learning, the two of you are constantly being elevated, and there is no end of your rise in HIM in sight. People in purpose feel purposeful. People in purpose are happier, and they are healthier. People in purpose radiate with a light that is unmistakably the light of GOD.

No matter where you are, and no matter where your wife is, you need to lead the both of you in CHRIST. You can change for the better, and your wife can change for the better. You just have to make up your mind to advance in CHRIST and refuse to retreat.

Talk to your wife, and the two of you should come together to set up some walls around your marriage. What's been a major issue in your marriage? Build a wall between it and your marriage. You do this by talking about it, resolving the issue before you leave the meeting table, and agreeing that the problem is no longer a problem. It is now a history lesson. For every issue that you have ever had in your marriage, take the time out to build a wall to keep it from entering your marriage again. Just because the problem is silent doesn't mean that it's absent.

Sometimes silent problems do more damage than problems that make themselves known.

Agree on disciplining the children. This is a problem in many homes because, as women, we often want to protect the children from Daddy because we feel like Daddy has heavy hands. But, this is division in the home, and it has to be kicked out. You have to both agree on how discipline will take place, and agree not to come against one another when a child has misbehaved.

Agree on your finances. This is another major issue, because oftentimes the wife wants to do one thing with the money, and the husband wants to do another thing with it. Ask GOD to make you better stewards over money. When Jean and I moved back to the United States, my mind was so accustomed to being in bondage that I clowned and cried when he refused to rent to own some furniture. I wanted to just pay monthly because we couldn't afford to buy it outright. I was so contentious back then, and I didn't trust his lead. Nevertheless, he refused to rent furniture no matter how much of a show I put on. He kept telling me that if we couldn't buy it outright, we weren't going to have it. He is completely against rent to owns, borrowing, etc. But, my life before Jean was completely different. I purchased a lot of furniture by signing my name on the contract and paying for it monthly until it was paid out. Jean refused to do this, and we had to sit on the floor and sleep on an air mattress for about six months. Nowadays, I am so very happy that he did what he did, because we are able to live comfortably now that we have furniture and no monthly bills except utilities. Now, I can NEVER go back to monthly bills because I've grown accustomed to being free of the bondage associated with loans.

Agree on friends and family. Remember this: Never let ANYONE place a divide between you and your spouse. Listen to one another in relation to your friends and family members. A show of respect for your spouse's wishes will always ignite a positive sequence of actions that will eventually become a lifestyle for the both of you. When Jean saw that I stopped placing people before him, he stopped placing people before me. I learned to stop telling him what I wanted and just be to him what I wanted from him. In doing so, he started reciprocating my behavior, and this soon became an unspoken law in our home. Be to your spouse who you want them to be to you.

Agree to serve the LORD and let HIM plant you in a church that you can be fed the uncompromising WORD of GOD often. Don't just attend churches religiously, refusing to go anywhere else because you don't want to offend the people there. That's error, and that's idolatry.

Just learn to agree with one another, but to do this collectively, you must both learn to agree with GOD. HE is not divided in HIS ways, so in agreeing with HIS WORD, you will agree with one another.

www.ingramcontent.com/pod-product-compliance
Lightning Source LLC
Chambersburg PA
CBHW060112050426
42448CB00010B/1852